THE
GRACIOUS
CALLING
OF
THE
LORD

THE
GRACIOUS
CALLING
OF
THE
LORD

ROBERT JOHN VERSTEEG

ABINGDON PRESS
NEW YORK
NASHVILLE

THE GRACIOUS CALLING OF THE LORD

Copyright © 1960 by Abingdon Press

Library of Congress Catalog Card Number: 60-10913

Scripture quotations unless otherwise noted are from
the Revised Standard Version of the Bible and are
copyright 1946 and 1952 by the Division of Christian
Education of the National Council of Churches of
Christ in the U.S.A.

SET UP, PRINTED, AND BOUND BY THE
PARTHENON PRESS, AT NASHVILLE,
TENNESSEE, UNITED STATES OF AMERICA

PREFACE

This book will serve its purpose if it helps the Christian evangelist to a fresh appraisal of his work—how evangelism inheres in the nature of the gospel; the favorable and the unfavorable forces and processes with which he must deal; the measures for choosing, discarding, or discovering techniques; what evangelism intends to accomplish. If it should also perform the more basic work of encouraging the reader in his examination of his own condition and his own response to the good news God speaks in Christ, then I am more than satisfied.

Evangelism concerns everyone. It is too much to hope that this study will directly reach the formally uncommitted and unconnected person, although I do hope that should such a one take it up either from curiosity or wistfulness he will find it worth his time. Lacking that opportunity, I have addressed myself to those who may relay to others whatever is valid in this message—to laymen and ministers who take up the work of evangelism, which ideally means all Christians. This book is the work of a minister who is persuaded that modern theology will speak with integrity and effectiveness in the life of the parish; that no gap between the two is necessary or permissible;

that ministers and laymen do not have to—and had better not—shift their minds into neutral when they practice evangelism day by day in the local church and community.

My thanks are due the many friends with whom I have shared in the work of evangelism in the parish. In lectures delivered at Garrett Biblical Institute, George Docherty dramatically opened to me the rich possibilities for studying evangelism through New Testament case histories. Richard Miller, then on the faculty of that school, encouraged a small group of men in the study of creative evangelism.

I greatly appreciate the help I have received from members of my family in the writing of this book. My mother volunteered to ready the manuscript for publication. My wife Sally has constantly been a gay, heroic feminine version of Horatius at the bridge. The greatest debt of gratitude is to my father, John M. Versteeg, who with tireless good humor pummelled my work with the medicine ball of criticism to toughen my ideas.

I wanted to write a book helpful to my fellow workers and worthy of the Lord's gracious calling. I am painfully aware how far I have missed that target, but I cannot think of another aim worth the effort.

—ROBERT JOHN VERSTEEG

CONTENTS

9

PART
ONE

THE INVITATION

THE CONVIVIAL CHRIST

Take up your forks and follow me!

Shall this be today's call to the Christian life? In a way, yes. Whoever loves a party, a banquet, a feast, may not be too far from loving the kingdom of God. The kingdom is not meat and drink, but the spirit of the kingdom certainly is the spirit of conviviality.

How many American church buildings will you find that have no dining facilities? The goal of most is to be equipped to dispense food for soul, mind, and body. Cupboard and choir, kitchen and classroom, counter top and Communion table—a nice balance is struck so that, in a manner of speaking, we have the pantry matching the vestry. Sometimes the former has the advantage. When you do come upon a church without kitchen or dining room you will see its people picnicking on the lawn or rearranging pews around tables in the sanctuary. Church suppers and Sunday-school socials are forever popular.

But not with some clergymen. We can sympathize with their dim view. It might be disturbing to subtract from the number who tuck napkins on Saturday night the number who stay tucked in on Sunday morning, the number of sinners saved in a year from the number served at supper. We can understand how the spiritual shepherd might be tempted to imagine Jesus speaking Upton Sinclair's words in rueful evaluation of his novel *The Jungle:* "I aimed at the public's heart, and by accident I hit it in the stomach." I have met men who actually considered themselves benefactors of the church because they patronized its banquets—low prices, good food, and no tips making victual virtue its own reward. Come, let us sing unto the Lord a new song: "When the rolls are served up yonder, I'll be there!"

What we caricature is the lopsided perversion of a persistent biblical triad: food, fellowship, and faith. Held together in the Bible generally, these three are shown together in Jesus particularly. "A man of sorrows and acquainted with grief," he was also a man of parties and acquainted with gaiety. Some were offended by this convivial Christ. They called him "glutton" and "wine-biber"; they criticized his choice in cup companions and declared it disgraceful behavior in a "holy man." Yet no scenes are more authentic, no settings more revealing of his personality. How natural for Jesus to be the center of a happy gathering! How perfectly in character for Jesus to choose his own companions and to bestow himself on sinners! What his critics condemned as scandalous Christians consider glorious.

In feasts Jesus finds an image which he often puts into simile, metaphor, parable, and practice to portray the kingdom of God. He makes a meal the distinctive act for those who belong to him; his identity is revealed to disheartened disciples when he breaks bread with them (Luke

24:30); he is recognized by others as he cooks breakfast for them (John 21:12). The evangelist will want to remember that the invitation which he is commissioned to extend was treated by his Lord as an invitation to a feast. In these pages, therefore, we shall draw near for a closer view of the tables graced by Christ. We shall find that Jesus has a genius for geniality. We shall make an approach to understanding what his invitation is, what it involves, and what it does. We shall watch men who refuse and men who accept his invitation, and we shall see the methods, the motives, and the consequences of their choices. We shall ask what meaning all this has for us and our practice of evangelism.

What does Jesus' comparison of the kingdom to a feast say about the nature of kingdom-life? [1] It says that the kingdom-life to which Christ invites men is an intimate fellowship gathered by the grace of God in which God's spirit is freely revealed, experienced, and appropriated.

The feast image shows first that Christ's kingdom is one of conviviality. Although the word has been used to connote a debauch—and some found that it suited their needs to apply that corrupted meaning to Christ—debauchery is only counterfeit conviviality. When we use the word we should think of a feast or an entertainment; of eating and drinking and the accompanying fellowship; of something social, something jovial, something gay. Here we use the word literally to mean "living with," and to say that guests are to be glad sharers-in-life. To be part of the kingdom means to share the God-ruled life of Jesus, and it also means cheerfully to share life with others. At

---

[1] Hoping that it may carry fewer stale connotations, I have preferred to use the phrase "kingdom-life" in place of John's equivalent "eternal life."

the Lord's table conviviality is never just between host and guest but among all, for Jesus makes it clear that the only way to share in his life is to share in the life of mankind.

God keeps open house. One of our young people's prayers is to "catch something of the sweep of [Jesus'] dominating dream of the kingdom of God." The sweep of its inclusiveness is unbounded, utterly lacking the restrictive qualifications men employ. Those of us who go about jangling the keys to the kingdom of heaven are in for a surprise—heaven has no locks. That realization is itself the key to kingdom-life. Therefore, insofar as the Church exists to demonstrate kingdom-life in its own fellowship, be certain that if there is any "outsider" to a church his name is Christ. Jesus always stands outside a fast-closed door. Insofar as the Church exists to redeem the world, it dare foster no separations either within or from that world. We may emphasize in this connection that Christ's calling is, at one and the same time, all-inclusive and yet specific to each individual; and if it is not really specific, then it is not really all-inclusive.

Mankind shares one common habitation. When there is a space ship in every garage that fact will only be written larger and underscored. We live in one universe—oneness being the accurate religious assumption in that startling word *uni*-verse. Now that we are invited to consider the prospect of sharing death like so many fish in a polluted stream, we are acutely aware that we share one atmosphere and that the choice has become conviviality or a common grave. Willy-nilly survival dictates that we must be, while salvation requires that we joyfully desire to be, sharers-in-life. Christ's life of fellowship is the one life suited for a world which makes us fellows in fact. If this is at stake, then the work of evangelism is urgent.

A second characteristic of the kingdom feast is companionship. Again we reach for the root meaning of the word: a companion is "one who shares bread." As God's guests we share in his largess. The earth's fullness is not ours to parcel out, to withhold, or to use for bribery; it is his, given us to share as stewards with the other guests.

The ritual of the Last Supper may have been separated from the fellowship meal because abuses arose—perhaps distortions similar to the misuses of our own church suppers. The early Corinthian Christians failed to share in the life of Christ when they failed in the sharing of food. "When you meet together," Paul wrote them, "it is not the Lord's supper that you eat. For in eating, each one goes ahead with his own meal, and one is hungry and another is drunk. . . . When you come together to eat, wait for one another" (I Cor. 11:20-21, 33). They had put the Lord out of their supper when they gave priority to satisfaction instead of to sharing. So with the kingdom-life. If the platter is passed to us first, it is not because we are greatest, nor is it so that we may have the greatest amount, but, rather, that we may become great by serving others. No more than we may use our trust as a threat or a bribe may we accept thanks for it as our due, thus feeding our pride on our own generosity. But in the sharing we may experience the gift of God. New Testament scholars suggest that the deeper meaning of the Lord's Supper is revealed in that moment when Jesus distributed the bread and wine. It is this act of distribution which gives impact to the words, "This is my body." Because to say, "Life is to be shared" is to say, "Bread is to be shared"; because the spiritual lives in the physical, kingdom-life is the life of brothers-in-bread.

Moreover, it is the shared life of reaching ever higher on the Lord's table for what is yet to be grasped—always filled, never satiated, urged upward by a foretaste of glory.

Jesus' image of the feast becomes still richer when he blends it with the symbols of a wedding: "The kingdom of heaven may be compared to a king who gave a marriage feast for his son" (Matt. 22:2); "Then the kingdom of heaven shall be compared to ten maidens who took their lamps and went to meet the bridegroom" (Matt. 25:1). Jesus not only calls to mind the picture painted by such prophets as Hosea and Jeremiah of the relationship between God and man as a marriage, but he weaves it of the stuff that life is made of and then sets the tapestry into iridescent motion.

The first-century Palestinian Jew knew no more high-spirited events than the wedding procession and feast. Everything else yielded—even a funeral cortege had to halt when the wedding party went by. Every man who met the bridal parade was expected to turn about and join in. Presents of wine, oil, and nuts were given to people along the way. Some of the celebrants carried bouquets, some bore torches, while still others held lamps set high on poles. It was a gala pageant of music, color, and dancing lights. Jubilation continued at the sumptuous wedding feast where gaiety was the order of the day—and night. Even soberly bearded rabbis were known to add to the hilarity with their famous humor, sometimes with less restraint than "piety" might prescribe.

This is what the word "wedding" meant to Jesus' hearers: merriment at the pledge of lifelong love and loyalty. When he chose this as an image for the kingdom of God, he was expressing the basic insight that kingdom-life is life in which holiness takes happiness by the hand. They go together. His purpose was to say that those who are invited to the kingdom are invited to be sharers-in-celebration.

Jesus was convinced that to be part of the kingdom is to be a participant in joy. Glad tidings are shouted in the streets. Every man ought to turn and join in happiness. Let one sinner swear allegiance to God, says Jesus, and all heaven breaks loose. Angels leap for joy. The tongues of men say it, too. Colloquialism's favorite phrase for a hilarious good time—"kill the fatted calf"—was Jesus' word for God's running welcome of a returning son. The Prodigal came home "and they began to make merry" and passers-by could hear the music playing.

Can our evangelism sound this note in a desperate world? Not pollyanna's tin-pan tune, please! The Master was also a man of sorrow, sad when a rich young ruler refused to join the line of splendor, tender with bereaved friends, moved to tears over his nation's capital city with its unlistening streets. He could drain a bitter cup and bleed and cry out from the cross. But in him every note of pain braced against a counterpoint of profound joy until the two strains merged into a chord at once tragic and triumphant. We dare not attempt to substitute for this the tinkling melodies of "jukebox religion." Neither may we suppose that we are hearing the hymn to joy in response to our evangelism when we mistake for the songs of convivial companions thronging up the steeps of light what is only the contented lowing of a herd gathered in baptized gregariousness to graze indifferently within the same pasture. The joy of those going to the kingdom feast must be something more than a matter of meeting each occasion with the decorous mood—in season grave, in season gay. And it must be much more than the frivolity of those fourteenth-century monks who relieved the tedium of long services of worship by dripping hot candle wax from the upper stalls onto the shaven heads of the singers in the stalls below! Jesus' joy is an underlying and overarching set of the spirit which has access to the fountainhead of life. His is not the ghastly grin, mocking grim fact; his is the steadfastly happy heart rooted in reality and seeming to sense the presence of God in the very midst of the starkest tragedy. He knows that however mightily the forces of evil trample earth with usurping step, God has not abdicated. He is the man of absolute faith in the accomplished triumph of the God who is love; and to participate in that victory is, for him, cause for celebration. Then let the rejoicing brought about by our evangelism be the rejoicing of a strong man about to run a race, let the songs of the saved be battle hymns, let the music of our gospel be not the jazz of an emotional jag but the exalted psalms of spirits praising our God who is abundantly able to save.

If we accept Christ's figure of the kingdom as a feast, then the invitation that the evangelist is to extend does not call men away from striving humanity to a drab life apart. Rather, it is a call into the life of mankind; a call to the endless challenge of the business of God's world, the shaping, the handling, the use of all its goods; a call to the high-singing mood of those who hunger with an unappeasable appetite for unattainable food.

> Ye nations, bend, in reverence bend;
> Ye monarchs, wait His nod;
> And bid the choral song ascend
> To celebrate our God.
>
> —H. KIRKE WHITE

2

INVITATION TO PARTICIPATION

Americans, the world's best builders of exteriors, should well be able to understand how a man may suffer inside. Many a pastor ministering to the inner wounds of his people has had cause to reflect on the ironic fact that nightmare lives may be lived in dream houses. Dinner jackets and evening gowns may be gay shrouds for misery; cosmetics may paint a glamorous disguise over spiritual leprosy.

Words of grief and loss-sharing are not to be taken at face value, of course; but there is something strangely revealing in that funeral parlor gambit: "Doesn't he look natural?" Someday some tactlessly literal person—I am always afraid I will be the one—is going to answer, "He looks dead to me!" The trouble is that it describes many who are not physically dead. For them it is an all-too-appropriate last word: never mind what he actually is; doesn't he look natural? That challenge and the importance of having a "nice-looking" casket cap frustration with foolishness. We are unparalleled architects of whitewashed tombs to hide away the undead—and often our religion is nothing more than a mortuary statue decorating the entrance, while walled inside the mausoleum a living soul, its cries of horror smothered in unheard echoes, dies.

Is there a more bitter way of being "lost"? It is similar to the plight of the accident victim who appears unhurt and who dies from internal injuries while the ambulance squad treats those with superficial but obvious abrasions. This was also the plight of Matthew the tax collector when Jesus came to invite him to abundant life. Matthew's condition illuminates the predicament of the contemporary man which our own evangelism must address. Evangelism in depth must be directed not only to the man suffocating inside the whited sepulcher, but also to every condition which brings about his imprisonment.

It is easy to see what Matthew's fellow Jews hated about the system of Roman taxation: the hardship it worked on them; the graft; the occasion it gave opportunists for personal gain through the collection of "public" funds; the foot-on-neck relationship it signified; and, most galling of all, the knowledge that taxes bled from "God's people" went to fatten a demonic government, Rome.[1] As events proved, the question of the tribute coin was politically and religiously as explosive an issue as could have been put to Jesus. If the problem of the ethics of payment—about which a man seemed to have little choice—was so loaded, then how strong the feeling against any Jew who took part in the collection! Small wonder that the Pharisees who were

---

[1] That subject peoples may have derived real benefits from the Roman government, that God may have been using the Roman state to work out his purposes in spite of the Romans' intent—such facts and faith indicate the complexity of the situation but do not immediately alter it. Taxes fed demonic elements in the state with wealth which belonged to God no matter whose image had been stamped on it. Jesus' answer of the tribute coin is therefore crucial.

committed to a policy of separatism would have nothing to do with Matthew and would not even accept his tainted gifts of money for the poor. In addition to being ceremonially defiled, Matthew was politically a hireling for Caesar —a quisling, a collaborationist. Much more is involved than mere social disapproval of his livelihood: the way he earned his living cut him off from participation in the life of his people. In their eyes, surely—and probably in his own—this meant that he was separated from his people's covenant God. Perhaps Matthew did not care. Perhaps not passionately but sullenly he defied his critics: "*I excommunicate you!*" or only laughed or shrugged or never thought about it. If so, it only shows how vast his separation had become. For what greater isolation can there be than indifference? No matter who did the excommunicating or how he did it, Matthew's tax collector's booth, with the world streaming by its door, was like a prosperous tomb.

Matthew lived within a system of injustice. He may have been at the very base of the tax pyramid which was crushing his people, but "low man" that he was, he was nonetheless a part of it. He participated in it and derived material benefits from it. He was involved in a cruel and corrupt structure which he himself did not design—and of which, for all we know, he may not have approved. Quite possibly approval or disapproval did not enter into it at all; it was just there. In either event it was a scheme of things in which Matthew had no effective voice. He was simply living life as it was.

Evaluating traditional doctrines of sin, Edward Ramsdell writes:

There is a sense, indeed, in which we cannot help sharing in the guilt of others as we participate in the social structures which sinful men have built, yet, the solidarity of sin must be so understood as not to make any man guilty until he has given his assent, implicitly if not explicitly, by actual participation.[2]

How could Matthew help but participate? How could he help but assent? How could he help but share the guilt?

Suppose Matthew had been moved to raise his voice against the Roman state. At best he might have been ignored or, worse for him, penalized. Had he, motivated by moral scruples, left the system flat, his leaving might have constituted a demonstration of protest but probably would have had no more effect than his criticism. Another cog would have been slipped into his place. Had he tried while operating within the system to ameliorate its harshness, he could have expected again either to be punished or to be replaced with a "part" which would function "properly." The best—and in one light also the worst—he could hope to achieve along these lines would be a negative righteousness, a cold purity of protest, or a personalistic piety by which he could declare himself innocent from responsibility for injustice, disengaged from the system, and absolved of his share of guilt. By doing this he would have made himself most guilty by surrendering to a demonic desire for personal salvation at the cost of concern for the oppressed.

This last may have been the line of resistance taken by some of Matthew's critics. They may have sought to affirm their own lack of guilt by rigid adherence to righteous laws —seeking to justify their part by asking if it was not "lawful" to give tribute to Caesar. For his part Matthew

[2] Edward Thomas Ramsdell, *The Christian Perspective* (Nashville: Abingdon Press, 1950), p. 135.

no longer could creatively participate in the community established by that system of laws which condemned him. Thus the laws themselves had assumed greater importance than the relationships that they were made to serve. There is a vast difference between the man who accepts, even unwillingly, any sort of benefit or protection from a government and the man who forces him to pay for it; but it is a difference of degree and distance. In effect both are participants. But if Matthew or any other man could not help his involvement, could not help but share the guilt of participation, then how could he be held responsible for what he could not help, and how could he be charged with that guilt as his own?

Since Matthew, because of his employment, was avoided by his people as they would have avoided an unclean corpse, we may suppose that if he thought about these matters at all, he rationalized his involvement as necessary and there made an end to questioning. But so far as we know Matthew neither criticized, deserted, nor sabotaged the system. It was his bread and butter. The plan of taxation and the Roman government, or in their place some form of taxation supporting some government less than the kingdom of God, some social order in which he and his critics must live if they were to live at all—this scheme of things would go on without Matthew.

Jesus' invitation does not, cannot, cancel out Matthew's participation in sinful social structures. Rather, the invitation involves a radical change in the nature, objective, and meaning of Matthew's participation by revealing ultimate structures beyond these—a transformation so great that at the same moment that guilt becomes personal responsibility, it also ceases to be a gulf of separation and becomes the occasion of repentance. It is a renewal from conforming to "life as it is" to living in the midst of "life as it is" for the sake of life as it should be.

The man Jesus calls to the kingdom feast and the man today's evangelism must call is man-in-society. The Bible knows no other man; there is no other man. In that case, no more than it can deal in surface appearances can our evangelism whitewash society's sepulchers. Proper exposition of all the social expressions our evangelism must have would lead us beyond the specific purpose of this book. That is the point. The fact that such far-reaching matters are and must be raised by the calling of one man indicates clearly that Christ's invitation involves all of society.

For his participation in the tax structure Matthew found himself ostracized from the Jewish community. The Pharisees called him a sinner—and he was. By the circle they drew to shut him out he was to understand that he was divorced from God. Jesus bridged that gulf, however, and brought God's invitation to the man who was alone and apart.

Matthew's situation grips our interest because it has so many points of contact with our own. Across so many centuries, over the wrecks of so many civilizations come and gone, though he lives in what seems to be a totally different world, modern man can feel an almost haunting sense of identification with Matthew the tax collector.

To live at all, he must take part in fallen social orders which do not value him. He feels trapped in a maze of demonic structures, but he feels no personal responsibility for them. Provided he has a degree of philosophical sophistication, he may agree that those structures exist and persist as the social extension of sins just like his own. Yet

27

he may wonder whether, had he not been born into those systems and conditioned by them, he would have become such a man. Biblical belief about man has answered: yes; just as man even in a perfect paradise would make himself and not God the center of his life, so each individual man, not of necessity but inevitably, repeats the performance. Sin is not the result of man's conditioning but the cause of his condition.

While he suspects this truth, society assures him it is not so. How is a man to be held accountable for the sins of a system? He is not responsible. Like Matthew he has no effect on that machine at all. Let him leave it. He is not indispensable; no one is. He is merely a replaceable part. He is not guilty because he is not responsible.

A man may believe that he ought to love his competitor as himself, but when he is one of eight thousand on the night trick at the factory, it is a bit hard to see how he can be held responsible for the policy decisions of a corporation. Although the pilot of an atom bombing mission becomes the victim of a guilt complex and scientists who develop nuclear weapons express misgivings, others remote from high places blot out their guilt with today's universal solvent for sin: "I am not responsible." But at what price? To give up responsibility is to give up manhood. Only a free human being can be held responsible.

What meaning for his life could Matthew have found in the tax structure? Only that he was a thing of no importance. He was not guilty because he was not responsible, not responsible because he was not free, not free because he was not man. He was a replaceable part.

Contemporary man finds this to be peculiarly his own situation. He has no choice but to participate in social structures which tell him that the meaning of his life is that he is a nonresponsible standardized cog in machinery which he exists to serve. He is "good" as he gears into it, "bad" as he does not. No wonder the degrading suspicion of his own worthlessness disintegrates his sense of morality like an acid and persuades him that the tomb is all.

In Matthew Christ invited a man similarly involved and Matthew responded. "And he left everything, and rose and followed him." (Luke 5:28.)

To stop the story here, as we so often do, is to arrive only at a salvation-by-subtraction. It is to make it appear as if Matthew were called out of a sinful social structure which is itself left otherwise untouched. It is to imagine Jesus practicing a purely pietistic brand of evangelism, calling the individual sinner and ignoring the fallen orders of society. To stop at this point is to achieve a simplicity indistinguishable from stupidity, since the injustices and usurpations of the system continue and another is engulfed in Matthew's place. It is to imply by defect that God is less concerned for the man who will take Matthew's place at the toll gate, thus committing in the name of Christ the same blasphemy of acting as if men were nothing more than expendable parts. The New Testament does not—and our evangelism dare not—stop the story here.

Jesus called Matthew to a renewal. Renunciation was required. In no other way could the physical following take place. But the emphasis was not on "leave everything"; it was on "Follow me." Other tax collectors—perhaps Zacchaeus is an example—did not leave everything. What Matthew renounced was security in the system, its standards, its goals and meanings as absolutes. The divine calling is not away from, but through, the secular calling; not from participation, but to worth-while and meaningful participation.

If Matthew's leaving indicates anything, it is the priority of human personality over any institution or social structure. This is the key, for it is this idea alone that is the one continuously regenerative power in the world. All other revolution is but replacement and rearrangement, re-formation and not transformation, by which one order is established in place of another order, one tyranny supplanted by another tyranny. The "new" asserts its absolute right to be, its right to perpetuate its being, its right to demand that human personality be subjugated for the sake of its protection, and so far is no different from the old which made the same assertions. At last it, too, is replaced and everything begins again and nothing is really changed. Christ's insistence that social forms are to be made and remade for man is the fountainhead of unending revival.

Matthew was invited—he had a choice about this—to participate in a new structure that had invaded human society in the person of Christ. He became a member of a community in which he was no longer a cog with a catalogue number but a person with a name. This was a group that did not demand the obliteration of guilt by the submergence of responsibility (along with personal identity). It was a new society in which he even vicariously took responsibility for the world's sin on himself and found victory over it in the service of the one Lord who is among them as one who serves. He was called to understand himself as a member of this body—indispensable, irreplaceable as a hand, precious as a child to his Father. When he suffered, every other member would share his suffering; when one rejoiced, all would rejoice. In this body with ultimate purpose, he found new meaning for his life; in this redemptive body his own worth had been redeemed. For Matthew life was no longer a tomb; it had become the temple of the Holy Spirit.

If this is something of what Christ's invitation meant to Matthew, there is no need to marvel at his response of spontaneous joy. If our evangelism is to tap such gladness today, it must do more than hang homey curtains in mausoleums, or make dying men "look natural," or snatch one prisoner away that another may be substituted in his place. It must release contemporary man from the domination of principalities and powers and extend to him a "frolic welcome" to a new society—a society not of the world and conforming to it, but very much in it and transforming it. The evangelism practiced by the church today must heal the inward wounds and revive the spirits of men who have been used as things and valued for their precision in meeting the specifications of machinery. It must invite them freely to participate as members of the body of Christ in the world, serving the most creative of all purposes and having absolute value because loved by God.

With a message this relevant and with evangelism that takes the plight of modern man this seriously, it will be no impertinence to hail men with Christ's welcome: "Enter into the joy of our salvation!"

3

APPALLING GRACE

Pastor Brown is dining tonight with the Community Boasters' Club. The biweekly crisis is at hand. The president of the Boasters' Club,—"Ernie," says his lapel label— clamps a clubby hand on the parson's shoulder and in the tone of a conspirator whispers, "Reverend, will you say grace for us?" For this moment came he to the dinner.

Boaster Ernie clunks a knife blade against a water glass. The buzzing subsides. Heads bow. The Boasters, eyes dutifully downcast ("I'll get a fork in that salad before Brantwurst gets mixed up again!") do not know it, but Pastor Brown has a hand grenade up his sleeve and is now nervously fingering the pin. For to meet these occasions when the prayer is as insipidly conventional as the sprig of parsley on the Swiss steak, the good man has secretly concocted a special grace, a sort of spiritual Molotov cocktail. One day, he has often told himself, his nerve will be up and he will say grace like this:

Omnipotent God, vouchsafe to forget about blessing this food, since thou carest not what goes into a man but what comes out from his heart. We would invoke the blessing of thy presence among us, except that we must ask thee to mind thy manners if thou dost actually come to our banquet, because, well, look what happened at Pentecost. It is not, O Lord, that we have hard feelings against thee; it is just that our membership is restricted, and the kind of company thou wouldst bring with thee would not fit in. We are gathered together to feast, and not to have fellowship with thee and thine. So when we invite thee to be our unseen guest at table, thou must understand that thou art to be the unnoticed guest. Amen.

Should Pastor Brown blurt out his bombshell blessing he would liven up the party and drastically cut down on his free meals. Pastor Brown has caught the big idea in a big way: grace is upsetting.

As gladly as Christ's invitation is extended and as profoundly joyful as is its deep significance, it is also sharply disturbing. "No human feeling," wrote Victor Hugo, "can ever be so appalling as joy." What human experience can ever be so shocking as grace?

It is hardly stretching the point to say that the first church meeting was a church supper. Jesus and Matthew and a large company of tax collectors, friends whom Matthew had called in to help celebrate the grace he had found in Christ, were there. Their merriment was upsetting to the Pharisees who murmured: "Why do you eat and drink with tax collectors and sinners?" (Luke 5:30); "The disciples of John fast often and offer prayers, and so do the disciples of the Pharisees, but yours eat and drink" (Luke 5:33). But Matthew knew why. His life of impotent bondage had been disrupted by the entry of Christ. That was something to kick over the traces about.

Matthew and Pastor Brown knew it, and another who

found out that the Deity is a disturbing guest was Simon the Pharisee.[1]

A Pharisee knew how to give a party, too, but decently, in order, and with a due sense of propriety. At the dinner where Simon played host to Jesus all the ritual ceremonies would be in force, every item of protocol scrupulously observed; but it would be no spontaneous outburst of joy as Matthew's celebration had been. What was prescribed, Simon did. Nothing etiquette demands was lacking, but it was on a minimum basis. There was a coldness in Simon's courtesy; the wine was carefully measured; there was no overflowing cup. Everything proceeded according to schedule.

Then a harlot crashed the gate. Talk about a disturbance! All the extra cordialities Simon had withheld she in grotesque parody lavished on Jesus: expensive pure nard for anointing, tears and towel of her hair to wash his feet, and kisses. Simon sat stunned. No prophet, his guest, else he would have known better than to permit such a filthy creature to accost him.

If the woman was an unexpected guest, then so was Jesus, for he did the unexpected. He defended the woman's actions, even praised her for them, and forgave her her sins. Simon the Pharisee had planned an exclusive little soiree, but his guest of honor was inclusive. Gaping at the scene, Jesus' disciples should have learned what all his disciples must learn—that you cannot invite Jesus to your own private party and enjoy his presence unless your welcome includes all whom he will welcome. If the woman was an unwelcome guest, so was Jesus.

[1] The narrative used here is synthetized from Matt. 26:1-13; Mark 14:1-9; Luke 7:36-50; and John 12:1-8.

The disciples were upset, too, and they had cause to be indignant. Jesus, all unselfishness, asked nothing for himself and certainly not the waste of nard that might have been sold and its price used for the poor. The woman clearly misunderstood what service was appropriate to the Master.

The disciples protested, but it was too late. There kneeling at the feet of Jesus was the woman—weeping, humiliated, and self-humiliating. She had missed it all along the way. Outcast, sinner, prostitute, she had come to Jesus determined to make a libation of something precious only to see in the disciples' scorn that again she had done the wrong thing—poured out as a token of repentance what might have become a tangible fruit of repentance. When she most desired to do something pleasing in Jesus' sight, she did, instead, something displeasing. Imagine her confusion!

This gracious guest, Jesus! Should he reject her as Simon did or criticize her impracticality as the disciples did? With a gallantry never taught by courtesy but only by compassion, he said, "Let her alone. . . . She has done a beautiful thing."

Hearing this, his disciples should have learned what Jesus' disciples must always learn: criticism alone cannot create the standards to judge what is and what is not appropriate response to Jesus. The types of service acceptable to the Lord are not limited to the range of our understanding. They may vary as widely as human need, human make-up, human motive. And though it differ from our own response or even seem to outrage our intelligent ways of looking at things, what is acceptable to the Lord must be acceptable to us. We must test all things; but the test is Jesus.

In this specific case at Simon the Pharisee's—and it is always the specific case which is upsetting—by his nonadaptive behavior Jesus challenges: (1) a system of human gerrymandering with boundaries marked off by ritualistic purity; (2) Simon's measure of self-righteousness understood as an obvious and invidious comparison between himself and the woman; (3) the common-sense view of the disciples, their smug assumption that their understanding of the mind of Jesus was the only allowable understanding, and their consequent criticism of the woman for her act; and (4) the attempt to restrict God's freedom to be God of grace, of forgiving acceptance. In every instance, God's reality in Christ bursts the stereotypes in men's minds.

This case is typical. Invite Jesus and you invite a disturbingly gracious guest. For he unsettles the "peace" of any order based on less-than-God, he confounds any frame of reference which is constructed, as though on rock, on the sands of mere ritual form or reciprocal politeness, of simple common-sense formulas. He is no chameleon Christ, taking on the color of his surroundings; he is the vivacious Christ who brings life to the party. He is jarring because he is gracious.

William Sheldon wrote:

The correctional personality becomes *unadaptively* different in every social situation. To the outer world the person seems to lack consistency, being at one moment radical among conservatives, and a little later conservative with radicals. This is unquestionably the most universally hated person in the world.[2]

[2] William H. Sheldon, *Psychology and the Promethean Will* (New York: Harper & Brothers, 1936), p. 254.

There is a sense in which Jesus fills and then exceeds this description. His behavior is adapted to the kingdom of God and is therefore always radically revolutionary in the kingdoms of men. His life is surely not just a series of perverse reactions but, rather, is motivated by a single-souled loyalty. It is this which accounts for what seem to be inconsistencies. Although, or because, conformed to the kingdom of God, in each situation his behavior is definitely adapted to individuals—and with a startling directness. For these reasons it may not prove an overstatement to say that "unquestionably the most universally hated person in the world" is Jesus. He is clearly what is probably the same thing: of all persons in the world the most universally disturbing.

Even as the real presence of God would upset the pie cart at the Community Boasters' Club, and Jesus' compassionate cordiality jolted the practical patterns in his disciples' minds, so Jesus, when he brings his invitation, characteristically brings a sword of conflict. There is a kernel of truth in the accusation his enemies brought before Pilate: "We found this man perverting our nation, and forbidding us to give tribute to Caesar, and saying that he himself is Christ a king. . . . He stirs up the people" (Luke 23:2, 5). Yes, he was turning the nation from the path it was following, heading for destruction. Yes, he was forbidding them to give as tribute to Caesar what was God's. Yes, he was such a king as this world has never seen, announcing such a kingdom as this world has never seen. Yes, he was stirring up the people. It is also true that Jesus was a disturbing man and his enemies meant to be rid of him. Theirs was only the last of a series of invitations extended to Christ requesting the pleasure of his absence.

The Lord's call of grace is an invitation which either produces the disturbance of fear and hatred or else "disturbs us with the joy of elevated thoughts sublime."

Therefore, if the welcome which our evangelism wins for Christ in the halls of men is only the politely patronizing toleration granted an innocuous guest; if, when presented to him, men are unperturbed as in the company of one from whom they have nothing to fear and nothing to hope; if, when introduced to him, men find a conveniently accommodating guest instead of one who at any party represents God's party—in a word and dogmatically, if our evangelism fails to disturb, then it has failed to present Christ.

4

THE STRUCTURE OF THE INVITATION

Of what does the evangelistic invitation consist?

Jesus' invitation to Philip (John 1:43-51) is representative of the New Testament records of calling and shows the essential elements. From a study of it we find that in Christ God offers man a personal relationship defined on God's side by the word "grace" and on man's side by the word "follow."

1. *The gracious calling of the Lord.* "And he [Jesus] found Philip and said to him, 'Follow me.'" Hollywood is fond of the legend of "discovery"; Christianity calls the fact of divine discovery "grace," meaning, for one thing, that in any spiritual transaction God is the party of the first part and that he launches the encounter from his side. In finding Philip and all the others he sought, Jesus established a pattern for translating faith in God's gracious love into terms of human action. Following that pattern is the chief motive and meaning of evangelism.

What sort of entertainment shall we imagine is provided at the kingdom party? The question is not entirely frivolous. Religion—or at least evangelism—begins as a game of hide-and-seek. Antedated only by "apple, apple, who ate the apple?" this is pictured as the world's earliest game in the Garden of Eden: man hides and God seeks. Man never seems to weary of this sport and its variations. His cunning at devising new hiding places, his ingenuity in camouflage, his artfulness, his resourcefulness in locating new blinds to secrete himself from God—all his craft in concealment he has perfected through the years.

In pages to come we shall watch the designs of his evasive action and probe for the reasons beneath it which have driven him at last to succeed in hiding himself so well that even he cannot find himself and is lost and unknown to himself. But God comes running in love—indefatigable and never-failing love. And he seeks man out. Hounded by heaven, man hides. The gospel is that God finds man.

God's invitation, then, comes enclosed in the envelope of God's gracious love. His "love that wilt not let me go" is in my hand before I open and read and repent. The stupendous fact that the invitation is extended to me at all is cause enough for rejoicing because it pledges God's willingness to welcome me. This is the way our evangelism must address men. Once let a man recognize himself as the object of God's seeking love and he is a marked man.

2. *A personal relationship.* This particular meaning can be heard if we stress the proper nouns and pronouns in repeating the invitation: "He found Philip and said to him, 'Follow me.' " The invitation is phrased in direct discourse; it is spoken person-to-person. And in this case that implies not long-distance calling, but no distance at all.

Much of what is passed off as "personal religion" is the cheapest kind of standardized, mass-produced, impersonal cant. Perhaps that and the modern obsession for anonymity partly account for its popularity. So often have the words become a verbal idol to which assembly-line saints bow down that we must think twice before using the term "personal Savior." Jesus, we have confessed, is also Savior of the world: in him all creation attains coherence, salvation from jumbled meaninglessness. But second thought confirms us in our use of the phrase because there is no cosmic Savior if there is no personal Savior. This is the point of the familiar story about young John Wesley, who said he knew Jesus to be Savior of the world and was then asked, "But do you know him as *your* Savior?" In the words, "Follow me," Philip is invited to a personal relationship— or more accurately, Philip is invited to a Jesus-to-Philip relationship with the Shepherd who calls his sheep by name.

This truth is missed—sometimes intentionally—by attempts to follow the "teachings" of Jesus, the "way" of Jesus, the "truths" enunciated by Jesus, or even the "idea" of God revealed in Jesus. This most modern of ancient heresies, the attempt to dehydrate divinity, results in a wrong relation; and the truth—including the truths of the teachings, the way, the idea of God—is revealed inside the relation, and outside it, it cannot be known, much less followed. I may "love" and "be loyal to" an abstraction, but how can I enter into a creative relationship in which I am in turn, in which I am first, loved steadfastly by the abstraction?

The soul-thrilling claim of Christianity is that the man who lives in such a personal relationship with Jesus of Nazareth lives in a personal relationship with God himself. Long after Philip had become a disciple he pleaded, "Lord, show us the Father, and we shall be satisfied." What asking!

41

And what an answer: "Have I been with you so long, and yet you do not know me, Philip? He who has seen me has seen the Father." (John 14:8, 9.)

"Knowledge of God," said William Temple, "can be fully given to man only in a person, never in a doctrine, still less in a formless faith, whatever that might be." [1] Jesus is that person pre-eminently. That is why we cannot in our evangelism say, "only believe," "have faith," "follow his way, his teaching, his example"; Jesus himself says, "Believe in me; I am the way, the truth, and the life." This is why in all our insistence that evangelism have content we must remember that its primary content can be nothing less than the person of Christ in whom God is reconciling the world to himself. Doctrines and disciplines may come also, but they come after and they come from him.

Present-day evangelism is much concerned with the problem of communication—and with good reason. For at bottom the problem of communication is the problem of bridging and overcoming the distance between persons, of revealing oneself—or something of oneself—to another. Our interest in communicating the gospel—a modern synonym for evangelism—is contemporaneous stress on the importance of that personal quality which is implicit in our faith about the Incarnation. In the words we speak and in every other form of self-impartation we hope to communicate to men not ourselves, but the very Word of God, Jesus Christ, in whom God reveals himself to man without other mediator.

According to Martin Luther, "The heart of religion is

[1] William Temple, *Nature, Man, and God* (London: Macmillan and Co., Ltd., 1949), p. 321.

42

in its personal pronouns." There also is the heart of discipleship and evangelism.

3. *Rise up and follow thee.* Nathanael responded to the enthusiasm of his friend Philip with the famous challenge, "Can any good come out of Nazareth?" Philip countered: "Come and see!" He had followed the pattern of Jesus' searching love by seeking out his friend, and now he rephrased Jesus' own invitation, "Follow me," which means, "Become my disciple, my daily companion. Come—and see." This—"follow me"—is the classic New Testament formula and very probably a verbatim report of the Master's own words, which must have been unforgettable to those to whom they were addressed. And this—"follow me"—spells out the nature of the relationship with God in Christ to which man is invited. These words tell us everything that is required of us; and these words require of us everything.

A man says he cannot follow Christ because he cannot believe in the accuracy of this or that statement about Jesus which he thinks the church requires him to accept. He cannot believe, for example, the very thing which we have been saying, that God is in Christ. But Christ says only (but mark that "only"!) "Follow me." The beliefs of the church have grown out of a relationship of following. They are formulations of that truth which can be experienced only in the corporate life of discipleship. We err if, in our evangelism, we give such a man cause to imagine that these results of following are either reasons or requisites for discipleship. We do not belong to the Christian family because we believe; we believe because we belong—and we cannot believe unless we belong. We do not follow Christ because we believe in him; we believe in

Christ because we follow him—and we do not believe unless we follow. Napoleon's aphorism applies with a different sense and a deeper meaning: "You commit yourself, and then—you see!"

Almost invariably this is the gospel order: first follow, then you will believe. The relationship is not primarily intellectual or creedal, nor even based on reverence or regard. It is simply, "Follow me." The following leads into all truth, for to follow is to be true. Thus,

The truth of Jesus Christ is not one truth among others; it is *the* truth, the universal truth that creates all other truth as surely as it is the truth of God . . . to know him is to know all.[2]

If kingdom-life is likened to a feast, then we may say that discipleship may be likened to a "progressive party." Is there a man whose social stock is so low he has never been invited to one of these meandering meals? It is great fun, trooping from house to house for course after course. Where is the party? Why, the party is in the pilgrimage. Accepting the invitation is the first step; but there is a long way to go, and there are many places to go, before the dinner is done. So Sören Kierkegaard can insist: "The proof of Christianity really consists in the 'following.' . . . There is only one way of being a Christian—to be a disciple."

The forms which following may take may vary freely from time to time, place to place, man to man. Following may be the "one way of being a Christian," but there are innumerable ways of following, just as there are countless

[2] Karl Barth, *Dogmatics in Outline* (New York: Philosophical Library, 1949), p. 59.

ways of staying or straying and being lost. By his refusal
to set narrow limits and definitions to "following" or to
route all traffic down one beaten path, the evangelist insists
on allowing the Holy Spirit freedom for his creative work.
If anything, he will encourage new departures in new
areas of discipleship, for he knows that no one follows
Christ in lock step. Following may require one type of
activity from me and quite a different sort of activity from
you; from either of us it may claim still another form of
activity tomorrow. The preposition "from" is important.
Whatever the form of following, it is called forth from us,
not imposed on us. Following is not walking "in his steps"
if that means that a man has only to plant his feet in so
many prints in some sort of spiritual Grauman's sidewalk.
We are not called to slavishness, but to liberty. We are
to follow the person as persons—spontaneously. Perhaps I
need more steps than you. Perhaps I have set out from a
different point. Perhaps I cannot run but only plod. But
in all our attitudes and projects we both may authentically
and personally, although differently, follow our Master.
The evangelist can offer no step-by-step blueprint for
Christian living, but he can give assurance of a daring
person to follow. Although both the problems of living
and the specific answers may change, the relationship of
leader-follower—that recreation which was the purpose
of seeker-hider—remains and shall remain constant.

This inward source of the patterns of following suggests
to us that while no other word fits it better than "follow,"
we must not permit this way of describing our response to
make us think that the direct, person-to-person relationship gives way to distant pursuit. The dedication of the
follower is matched with a devotional sense of the presence

of the leader. Christ goes on before and yet is closer than breathing. For grace, which means that God finds us in our need, also means that he goes with at the same time that he leads. Christ's invitation is simultaneously the pledge of his own presence, and it contains the promise that he will never fail to be true to that relationship.

The experience of Frau Anna Gunther is in pattern a near-perfect analogy to this nearness of himself which Christ offers in his invitation:

Around April 1945, we were in a school at Konigshof, in Czechoslovakia, when the order came to evacuate because the Russians were drawing near. We started at 2 o'clock in the morning, in the dark, each doing as best he could. As I could not walk very far, because I am already 70 years old, I had to stay behind. . . . It was afternoon and about four o'clock, and all the others had long since gone on. I had taken my shoes off and was walking in my stocking feet, but I could not go on and sat down at the roadside . . . and thought I must just leave myself in the hands of the Lord. It was not long before a Czech came by . . . and took away my bag. . . . After a while an American Negro soldier . . . came towards me and I thought my end had come. He came straight up to me and said "Now Ma, can't you get along?" "No," I replied. He took my hand and helped me to get up, put on my shoes, and then gave me his arm to help me along. We went a little way and came to a village where there was an inn. He put me on a bench under the trees. . . . He soon came back with a cup of coffee with sugar and cream, and a buttered roll and said "Now get your strength up again and then we'll go on, I patrol as far as the frontier." [3]

[3] *Documents of Humanity*, K. O. Kurth, compiler (New York: Harper & Brothers, 1954), pp. 22 ff. Used by permission.

"I patrol as far as the frontier"—even unto the end of the world.

Our examination of the calling of Christ has shown us something of the nature of the life to which man is invited: its conviviality, companionship, and note of celebration; its scope and sweep—all-inclusive, intensely personal, and at the same time radically regenerative in society. We have seen the disturbance caused by the invitation either because it offends or because it exalts with its call to live the will of God in the world of men, and the gracious relationship which the invitation at once signifies and offers for man's appropriation. The invitation is God's; the decision is man's.

Let us now attempt to clarify our understanding of this act of decision and the dynamics with which evangelism works.

THE STRUCTURE OF DECISION

5

THE STRUCTURE OF DECISION *

Decision operates when a person becomes aware of alternatives regarding which he can and must exercise choice, creating in him the consciousness of freedom.

As we look in this chapter at five elements of the structure of decision under the headings *Possibility*, *Will*, *Necessity*, *Time*, and *Freedom*, we will have to remember that it is like hearing the sections of an orchestra rehearse their parts one by one. We make our division only for the sake of clarity. We are not here examining the living process of decision itself—that is, the actual making of the choice—which will become our concern in the remaining sections of this book. Here we are reconnoitering the battleground on which the struggle takes place, the field of forces within which choice is made. To give it the concreteness which decision must always have, we draw our analysis

---

* This chapter's course is set through deep waters with complex cross currents. For the sake of pursuing its purpose more directly, the language of qualifying phrases and the consideration of more subtle relationships have been omitted. Not because these are unrecognized or unimportant, but simply because "in striving to be precise I become obscure."

from the New Testament record of the calling of Simon Peter (Luke 5:1-11; Mark 1:16-20).

POSSIBILITY

"Depart from me, for I am a sinful man, O Lord." In this echo of man's reluctance when confronted with the claims of the highest—"I am slow of speech"; "I am a youth"; "I am a man of unclean lips"—Peter says more about Jesus than about himself. His acknowledgment of sin is as full of faith as his following is to be full of sin. But he was probably less interested in his confession's accuracy and implications than in its intended effect— "Depart from me." The purpose of Jesus' words was to bridge distance; the purpose of Peter's words was to put distance between them. It is still life's biggest surprise: Jesus does not depart from, he comes to the sinful man and invites the sinner to belong to him. Is this the source of "that grave surprise that is the only real happiness that is possible to man"? Jesus does not withhold grace with all of its possibilities.

What had Peter imagined possible for himself? Against the screen of the future did his mind project images of himself as the moderately thriving owner of a small fishing fleet, an industrious family man, a responsible and respected member of the Jewish community? Christ presents a new possibility: "Follow me, and I will make you a fisher of men."

Mistaken for a salesman and asked what his wares were, Bishop Quayle flashed back the inspired answer, "I sell horizons!" Jesus before all others deals in that heavenly real estate. Our faith is that there are no boundaries and no limitations in the Christian vocation, that Christ is free to call any man whatever his condition and capabilities and to offer him all the possibilities of the kingdom.

In literal fact, Jesus offered Peter these immediate alternatives: remain as he was with all the same possibiltiies he had entertained as he was (except the possibility of making a positive initial response to Christ's invitation), or say, "Yes, I will become a follower." Here is the invitation: accept or refuse. Grace presents new possibility and God's love always demands decision.

WILL

The idea that a man can control a sequence of cause and effect and its final product is the idea of will. This is the decisive implement for the shaping of a man's life, since it is his power to choose what or whom he will follow. Provided that he is free, what a man follows indicates what he wills. Will is man's capacity to select direction, purpose, goal. It represents motive and, morally, motive is the man.

So complex are the skeins of life that any simple and cocksure reliance on the will as an effective factor in fate seems naïve. We may easily misjudge a decision's actual consequences. One way or the other we may miscalculate the weight of one man's will. We may to our regret ignore the principalities and powers against which the will must wrestle. On the other hand, any philosophy of futility that considers man to be a helplessly ineffectual pawn, determined and without self-determination, powerless to initiate, to interrupt, or to alter causative sequences which are the paths to destiny, must be examined with an eye to finding out whether this is not one more subtle attempt to escape the necessity and the responsibility for the risk of free decision, thus demonstrating its own falseness. Jesus recognized Peter's capacity for self-determination.

Peter's decision would have consequences. He was probably unable accurately to predict the exact end result, but he could choose his direction fully aware that his choice would bring its products. We, this side of the Cross, can see to what glory his first decision led; Peter could not read the testimony of history but only the testament of faith. Peter could not choose the experiences that would come to him; but he could and did choose the person in whose presence he would meet them. The faith that enabled him to follow had to be primarily faith in the person he decided to follow. The attraction was in Jesus. He was himself the aim of the chain of events Peter elected. Who can say what the magnetism was at that moment? Some flame in the Master's eye, the vision of one who has dwelt in mountain tops and beheld new horizons, the sound of a voice speaking as words of life things which before had been only dream dialogue—something in Jesus affected the actual operation of Peter's choice, but the capacity and the responsibility for making that purposeful choice lay in Peter.

NECESSITY

Jesus had said to Peter: "There is a choice and you are able to choose." But more than that, for Peter choice had become a necessity.

By necessity I mean first that quality in decision that arises from selectivity. Our small son Jack took a cap pistol and rubber tomahawk to a western movie. When the cowboys were on, he brandished his six-shooter and was Wide Burp, cowhand. When the Apaches whooped it up, in his other hand Jack flailed his tomahawk and became Big

Chief Popcorn-in-the-Mouth. In the finale's pitched-battle showdown, Jack excitedly waved tomahawk and pistol simultaneously. But we are never spectators of the invitation to the feast; we are always involved. Let me recognize a possibility as my own possibility, and choice has become for me a matter of necessity. I must choose, and I must choose some definite thing.

But self-determination is self-limitation, because every positive choice involves a corresponding negative choice. Peter might have had a "good" life as he was, but he had to surrender it in order to choose a better life. This is one root of the disturbance grace creates, since the possible self Jesus offers a man represents a threat to the self he has and to all other possible selves he had imagined as extensions of that old self.

When we go a step further we see that it is only through accepting self-limitation that we achieve self-definition. We define ourselves in and through our decisions—their negative side no less than their positive—just as we express meaning by selecting certain words from all those possible and just as the sculptor frees from a block of stone one actual creation, definite and real, at the cost of surrendering all other possibilities he might have seen in it. This is Peter's —and every man's—spiritual situation: choose to actualize one possibility, and in that same act you dismiss others.

Perhaps, as some have suggested, it is not always that a man wishes to retain the vast world of the possible so much as he dreads to obtain the world of the actual at the cost of confessing the limited nature of his existence—that is, his creatureliness. Decision with its self-determination and self-limitation defines the actual self from possible selves; a real self with all its risks and vulnerability, from no self. This can be profoundly disturbing.

You cannot get rid of this element of selectivity in decision. It remains in the structure even in the midst of attempts to deny or to overcome it. If Peter, or any man, attempts divided allegiance, he must give up the possibility of wholehearted following. But for Peter in the concrete scene before us, division was physically impossible. We do not have to suppose that Peter instantly attained that devoutly-to-be-wished state in which all his conflicts were consumed in one holy flame of single aspiration. He had to take his warring desires with him. Until he went to a cross in Rome he remained in the process of deciding, which is to say, he continued becoming truly man living by faith. When Jesus called him he was not yet a man of one will. He was a man of many minds, but only one body. Taken at its lowest term, the invitation is to walk after Jesus. So to the question, "Why did you follow him?" poet Andrew Young lets a disciple reply:

> I think it was our feet that followed Him;
> It was our feet; our hearts were too afraid.[1]

So far as his feet are concerned, Peter hears the invitation in such an unequivocal form that it is impossible for him simultaneously to follow and not to follow. However suspect a dichotomy may be in the world of logic, in Peter's experience of that moment the "either-or" was real. The simplicity of it is literally and necessarily Yes or No. Unless our own evangelism can at times reduce itself to this

---

[1] "Nicodemus," by Andrew Young; from his *Collected Poems*. By permission of Rupert Hart-Davis Ltd.

sort of stark necessity, it is eaten away by the self-deception of vagueness, the refusal to accept the risk of self-definition. The evangelist must stress these points of immediately relevant action. We cannot abstractly describe the content of such acts—walk with me, join this church, feed these hungry, vote for this legislation, do this piece of work—but we can and we must show definite movement in the world as inescapable choice and commitment.

In addition to the necessity which arises from selectivity among alternatives, there is also a second sort of necessity which springs from confrontation. Some sort of decision must be made.

Peter was once a nameless face in the crowd: the crowd came after Jesus; but Jesus came after Peter and with startling directness turned and singled him out: "This concerns you. I am making this your business. Whether you will or no, I am involving you." We will see the most important effect of this under the heading of *Freedom*—a necessary freedom to choose, a freedom Jesus is not content Peter should escape. Here we point out that it also has the effect of forcing the choice. Peter must do something—even if that something is nothing. If nothing is what he decides to do, his negative action will produce its own results. Only let him become aware of the possibility, and doing nothing has assumed the character of deliberate choice.

Time

The element of necessity is made acute because the structure of decision pivots on a concept of time. Peter was on the knife-edge of "now." Suddenly, immediately, he had to decide. Since we have spoken of will as the attempt to affect a causative sequence, we can also say that decision is dealing in futures now.

Christianity is chronically chronological. It claims that eternal significance is wrapped up in the fleeting moment, and thus "temporarily" is as important a word as the Christian knows how to use. With significant persistence Jesus speaks of the necessity for grasping the moment. He announces God and the kingdom in the present tense. The tempo is urgency, *subito:* the kingdom is at hand; the feast is prepared; the acceptable day is now.

With, from man's side, an inscrutable eternity hanging on the moment, Jesus demanded of Peter an instantaneous, daring response: at that particular moment Peter could either follow or not. To defer, to delay, is temporarily—I mean, inside of that moment which has eternal and not passing significance—to say, "No."

It may be, as I believe, that the door by which a man may enter into life is a revolving door which no one may shut. The secret of a revolving door is simple—seize the opening as it presents itself. Another opening may come with another moment, but—to update the ancient philosopher—you cannot step into the same revolving door twice, if not because it is a different or atomically altered segment of the door, then because you are a different person—different, for one thing, in that you are now a person who refused the first opportunity and waited.

It is not always readily apparent, and it is fantastically difficult to convince a man, in just what way the missed moment has eternal significance. In the case of the man who builds an inhibitory habit of hesitation or fear, the consequence is obvious—or should be. That someone in need of his help was to be reached through that door and was now lost because of his reluctance is not impossible to explain. But that each "now" is spiritually the full compass and range of eternity, a moment in which God can be known and thus a moment containing completion, seems arrant madness to one who tells time only by the tick of a watch. Such a man would scarcely appreciate the humor of that secretary who, when told by her impatient boss, "You should have been here at nine o'clock," asked, "Why? What happened?" And such a man can hardly appreciate the importance of the moment in which the fullness of life with God in Christ is offered. At any given moment of time, either a man follows Christ or he does not.

The element of time in the structure of decision should also warn us that new moments of time demand new decisions. Peter's decision at the harbor of Capernaum was the first in a series, some of which amplified and some of which subverted this one. It was the point of the wedge. This initial step was not to relieve Peter of further decision —the sort of relief sometimes alleged to be the "explanation" of conversion. Rather this was the decision without which his particular future decisions would not have had to be made. In at least this one sense it is true that "it is only the first step which costs" and, we might add, in this sense it is only the first step that counts, so important is the action in that moment.

It is not true that Peter stood at the crossroads, for the crossroads will not stand still. Peter was swept along escalator-like sidewalks at high speed; and time was a treadmill whirling alternate paths to his feet. Jesus had called him; Peter must either leap or be carried along willy-nilly. Beyond this crossing at coming moments is an intricate series of diverging networks, so that new possibilities to choose new directions, the necessity for ever new decisions, remain. "The choice goes on forever."

FREEDOM

We agreed that our division of the structure of decision into five conveniently labeled elements was to be only a device for study. I should not defend the division very strenuously if someone were to argue that there is no real difference here, as we discuss freedom, between the part and the whole. I would applaud the insight.

We are now at the central element of the structure of decision and the factor of the most crucial importance for the work of evangelism. For just as there is no sense in talking about decision unless we mean choice that is free, neither is there any real freedom without decision. This means, if Christianity is correct in understanding man as free before God, that man depends upon this decision for his very existence.

By the word "freedom" I mean here a man's ability to make his achievements, his actions, and his attitudes his own.[2]

Jesus, when he said, "Follow me, and I will make you a fisher of men," assumed that Peter was free to respond. Was he?

[2] The interrelatedness of these elements may be seen in that freedom stands as the subjective counterpart to objective possibility, and in quantity and quality is therefore relative to awareness of possibility. Freedom is not the result of, but the cause of the element of necessity, inasmuch as to say "I can" and "I may" is to say "I must." We have seen that there is a necessity for choice at the moment there is a possibility of choice. But this possibility is not real unless the freedom is real; and the freedom is not real unless the possibility is real. Also, if there is not freedom, then the notion of having the power to affect a causative sequence for a purpose is of no practical interest, since that power cannot then be applied as one chooses, cannot truly be one's own.

Peter was not free from the claims of society. Whatever inequities there were in the economic system of his day, Peter was taking something out of it and he was putting something in. We cannot imagine Jesus irresponsibly calling the entire fishing industry away from the harbor of Capernaum. Peter had an honorable if paltry part in the process by which life is sustained. The creation of wealth—or at least the extraction of it from the lake—was moral, satisfying, necessary work, even though a portion of the proceeds went through taxes for the support of emperor adoration. We are uncertain about the extent of Peter's family, but we know he was not free from some claims in that direction, and Jesus himself had fulfilled similar duties. Peter was not free from mankind.

Were there also interior pressures that limited Peter's freedom? What psychological determinants lay buried in his subconscious? What powers "lived" in him? Was he free from the grip of idols? From sin? He thought not: Peter claimed he was a slave to sin and as such not free to associate himself with Jesus. Jesus accepted the fact as if he had power to free Peter from the hold of sin. Neither was Peter free from his past. This decision was not independent but related to the choices that had made him the man he then was.

No. Peter was not free—not from all these pressures. Neither, he discovered in a new way in Christ, was he free from the pressure of God. He was confronted and Jesus demanded a response. Peter was not free not to be free to choose. Jesus presented the possibility and the necessity of choice and in that encounter Peter became free.

This is the reason why a laissez-faire policy in evangelism is not only unrealistic but inhuman and unchristian. It is equivalent to surrendering the field without joining battle, thereby depriving the soldier of his right to be a soldier since he can be a soldier only by joining battle. What could be more blind than to suppose that a man is free from pressures and conflicts? What could be more piously foolish than for the evangelist to refuse to exert pressure in man's behalf on the grounds that man ought not to be pressured? He is pressured—especially in our modern world of hidden persuaders. The climate of opinion, the very atmosphere in which a man must live exerts pressure on every square inch of his being. Freedom from conflicting pressures is guaranteed only by the unilateral pressure of totalitarianism, that is, by "freedom-from-freedom."

Sometimes a conscientious Christian will today recoil from bringing to bear the pressure of evangelistic confrontation, saying that such activity violates respect for personality. Quite the opposite. It is this refusal which truly disparages a person's dignity of decision, deprives him by default of the possibility of defining his personality through choice. This refusal also denies him his real freedom. We have said that as there is no decision without freedom, so there is no freedom without decision. And without either there is no real person. "Freedom," said my teacher, the late Edward Ramsdell, "cannot be understood apart from what the individual is, nor can what the individual is be understood apart from his freedom." [3] It is decision that creates man in his existence in freedom.

So much is true of choice in general. Because the alternative possibility Christ presents is radically different from that involved in all other choice—the possibility of gaining

[3] Ramsdell, *op. cit.*, p. 139.

victory over sin by existing as the forgiven child of God—therefore the freedom this particular decision creates is also radically different from all other, conditional freedoms. It defines life with respect to God.

The man who desires to be free from choice is the man who desires not to be man. Whoever would refuse to let choice be presented to another would refuse to let that other become man. Recognizing the truth in existentialism's theme "that the actual nature of our existence is known only through the free decision and risk of the human spirit in confronting our insecure and temporal life," [4] we can understand why Berdyaev can speak of "grace" as the inward illumination of freedom.[5] This grace comes to us in Christ. The pressure exerted by God in Christ, far from negating man's freedom, actually creates the possibility of it, offers freedom as an alternative from the pressures of sin. Freedom has been called "the power to become what we were intended to be." The truth in Christ creates that freedom, which remains, however, a "struggling freedom."

Peter was not free until Jesus found him. He could make his life his own only by choosing it. Man is created by the Word of God—free and free to become. And "this same freedom," to come full circle in the dynamic tension which cannot be resolved without destroying man, "forces upon men the necessity . . . of decision about the character and direction of his life." [6]

---

[4] Daniel Day Williams, *What Present-Day Theologians Are Thinking* (New York: Harper & Brothers, 1952), p. 125.

[5] *Modern Christian Revolutionaries*, Donald Attwater, ed. (New York: The Devin-Adair Company, 1947), p. 346 ff.

[6] Langdon Gilkey, *Maker of Heaven and Earth* (Garden City, N.Y.: Doubleday and Company, 1959), p. 193.

> This direction is possible for you.
> You can choose.
> You must choose.
> You must choose now.
> You are free to choose;
> > And in choosing you become free;
> > And in becoming free you be-
> > come free to choose.

This spiral of becoming is the organic structure of dynamic decision. This is the stuff of which life is made. This is the framework within which choice and evangelism operate. What response shall a man make to the words of destiny: "Follow me"?

> Why did you come, with your enkindled eyes
> And mountain-look, across my lower way,
> And take the vague dishonor from my day
> By luring me from paltry things, to rise
> And stand beside you, waiting wistfully
> The looming of a larger destiny?
>
> Why did you with strong fingers fling aside
> The gates of possibility, and say
> With vital voice the words I dream today?
> Before, I was not much unsatisfied:
> But since a god has touched me and departed,
> I run through every temple, broken-hearted.
> > —MARY WEBB[7]

[7] Mary Webb in *The Distaff Muse*, Clifford Bax and Meum Stewart, comp. (London: Hollis and Carter, 1949), p. 193. Used by permission.

PART
THREE

REFUSAL

6

METHODS OF REFUSAL

I fled Him, down the nights and down the days;
   I fled Him down the arches of the years;
I fled Him down the labyrinthine ways
   of my own mind.[1]

In the evangelistic symphony, the first movement after the overture is usually a fugue with variations. To pursue, to overtake, to intercept a fugitive from grace, the evangelist must study to know every byway and turning in the maze of escape down which the truant guest may take to his heels. Our procedure in this section will be first to observe techniques of refusal, then to examine reasons for refusal, and finally to suggest an underlying cause of which these are symptomatic.

In manner, refusal may vary from cordial noncommittalism to brutal violence. In method, the refusal complex presents a fascinating study in human ingenuity.

The rock-hard refusal—Saul's, for example—is in some

[1] Francis Thompson, *The Hound of Heaven*, stanza 1. By permission of Hollis & Carter Ltd.

ways the most hopeful of all, offering as it does the traction of open honesty. But in a culture in which it is considered bad form to be offended at Christ, you will seldom find a pure "No." The flat rejection is usually adulterated with a rationale, with the reasons being given less often in support of the "No" than of the man who uses them.

The garden variety of refusal is *evasion of decision*. The great percentage of other escape routes are only alleys within this subdivision. Strangely—or, if we accept the communications theory that awareness increases in proportion to unexpectedness, then not so strangely—in our world where partisans of Christ represent their Master on street corner, billboard, and bus, it is peculiarly easy for a man to evade making a response to the challenge, "Follow me," though of course the evasion itself is a negative response. We are not talking about Adam's simple avoidance, which is a popular but rather primitive—and on the whole, futile—form of flight. There are no doubt great numbers of men who attempt it. But in the present state of things it is like trying to avoid television. No, we are talking not about avoiding the confrontation, but about emptying it by evading responsibility. Avoidance is the denial of the possibility of the alternate way Christ offers and is usually accomplished by jamming or distorting the message or by smashing transmitter or receiver. By evasion, on the other hand, we mean the attempt to break down the structure of decision at the point of necessity. People who live in a schizophrenic society become agile matadors accustomed to dodging dilemmas, evading the horns, and grabbing the tail.

Refusal by evasion may be the denial that urgent cosmic issues are at stake or that, for good or ill, we are participants in that struggle. The apocryphal story goes that Heywood Broun looked over a long menu handed him by a restaurant waiter and said, "I see nothing to object to." This cartoon of vacant-minded expansiveness—which if Mr. Broun had ever indulged for the amusement of his dinner companions, he practiced nowhere else—is not quite so far-fetched when used to describe some men scanning the menu of religions. The kingdom feast is not the bland acceptance of everything without objection; it is choice of the meat and drink of life. Kierkegaard felt the meaning of Christianity to be "that a man should live his life in such a decisive way, should so definitely and openly maintain what he wills, what he believes and hopes, that it is impossible all might speak well of him." The end result of negative decision is nothing. George Orwell knew of a periodical which described itself as "non-political, non-educational, non-progressive, non-cooperative, non-ethical, non-literary, non-consistent, non-contemporary." [2] The life which lacks positive or selective decisiveness lacks definition and, lacking definition, does not ex-ist in the sense that it does not stand-out before God. Richard Armour's poem placards this disease of the undecided and undefined soul:

> The neutralist stands on the sidelines,
> Which for his sake we hope are wide lines,
> And cheers both sides with equal measure.
> (Impartiality's his treasure.)
> He cannot tell the wrong from right,
> Black always looks the same as white,
> And free and slave and gay and grim

[2] George Orwell, *A Collection of Essays* (New York: Doubleday and Company, 1954), Doubleday Anchor Books, p. 225.

> Are very much the same to him.
> So there he stands, all happy-sad,
> And waves his banner, which is plaid.[3]

Plaid souls! I cannot recall. Was the flapping banner followed by the wavering crowds in Dante's limbo plaid? I think it was. It should have been.

Back of this tartan attempt may lie a feeling of futility and hopelessness, or a kind of arrogance of independence, or a concern with self that, being with good reason afraid to risk itself, loses itself. The defiance and fear simply propel the eraser in a vicious circle and the result is a blank, an undefined dilettante, never committed to a cause.

Backed into a blind alley in the labyrinth of flight, evasion may assume the form of *substitution*. To the demand, "Follow me," the cornered soul makes surrender, "Yea, Lord, to the death I admire thee." It is disturbing to reflect that the forms of religious life may themselves abet this type of refusal. Where worship becomes a substitute, rather than the open floodgate, for following; where the tithe is offered not in token of, but in lieu of, redemptive stewardship; where membership in an organization is put in the place of sharing the life of an organism; this sort of proxy piety is a serious misunderstanding of what the grace of God requires in response. Substitution may be made for the term "me" and, as we saw when discussing the structure of the invitation, the challenge of Christ is then met with the answer, "Yea, Lord, to the death I follow thy way, thy teaching, thine example."

[3] Richard Armour, "The Neutralist," copyright 1956 by The Curtis Publishing Company. From *Nights with Armour* (New York: McGraw-Hill Co., 1958). By permission of the author.

We have already stepped onto those paths of escape wherein refusal is accomplished through acceptance. These are techniques for running away while staying at home, the sort of ability demonstrated by the Prodigal Son's elder brother. One of these is *conditional acceptance*—a limited response in the face of unlimited grace—in which a man attempts to dictate to God the terms of the invitation. Here the answer is, "Yea, Lord, I will follow thee so long as thou art 'going my way.' " This is a kind of hitchhiking toward heaven, a casual acquaintanceship struck up where paths coincide; but the concurrence does not outlast the coincidence. It is pilgrimage with the provisos: "This is where our paths part; this is as far as I go; this is where I get off." More seriously, those who go along for the ride may attempt to compel Christ to go their way, the mutineers may attempt to seize the ship and set their own course in the name of and under the flag of a captive Christ.

What reaction to Jesus is more persistent than the endeavor to clothe him in the cast-iron armor of our own ideas rather than to be, through him, clothed in our right minds? Persistent because so long as we are what we are, nothing else is possible for us. Mankind's most deadly disease is the stereotype, a mental graven image by which we see not what is there but what we expect to see. This aborts decision at the point of new possibility.

Pilate could not resist the temptation to make use of Jesus in order to serve his own interests with Herod. He did not understand that Christ's was to become the true revolution of regeneration and was not just a matter of some new tyrant's assuming the old marks and implements of the same power. What bitter mockery, then, when Pilate's soldiers impressed their idea of a "king" on this

Prince whose kingdom is not of this world, clothing him in purple robe and crowning him with thorns! Then, again, we have seen men strip the seamless robe from Christ and invest him with the seamy cape and hood, disguising the cross-bearer as a cross-burner. Once upon a time Jesus was given a silk topper and morning coat and sent out as a front man for laissez-faire capitalism; but the silk hat could not hide the awkward scars on his brow. To impede medical, social, and scientific advances, he has been decked out in the duds of the cleric, the lawyer, the judge, the colonial administrator. He has been slung with sandwich boards and shoved out to toddle up and down the streets advertising all sorts of bright ideas and minor fads. He has been conscripted—"After all, he is a citizen, isn't he?"— and issued the ill-fitting uniform of almost every nation fighting for almost every "cause." He has been dolled up like Little Lord Fauntleroy, sentimentalized and sissified. They have costumed our Christ in the cap and gown of the psychiatrist. They have washed the "hard sayings" from his mouth with soft soap and given him for utterance nothing but the slushy froth of common-sense slogans. It is our habit to dress him in our habit, to measure and fit Christ by the size of our own custom-made dummies, to avoid the glare and glow of his countenance by making Christ the man in the iron mask—a mask from our own forge!

Christ wears no man's livery; only God's.

George Bernard Shaw put his finger on this—or rather, he gleefully jumped on it with both feet in hobnailed boots:

You may deny the divinity of Jesus; you may doubt whether he ever existed; you may reject Christianity for [any other religion]; and the iconolaters . . . will only classify you as a freethinker or a heathen. But if you venture to wonder how Christ would have looked if he had shaved and had his hair cut, or what size in shoes he took, or whether he swore when he stood on a nail in the carpenter's shop, or could not button his robe when he was in a hurry, or whether he laughed over the repartees by which he baffled the priests when they tried to trap him into sedition and blasphemy, or even if you tell any part of his story in the vivid terms of modern colloquial slang, you will produce an extraordinary dismay and horror. . . . You will have made the picture come out of its frame, the statue descend from its pedestal, the story become real, with all the incalculable consequences that may flow from this terrifying miracle. . . . Thus it is not disbelief that is dangerous in our society: it is belief. The moment it strikes you . . . that Christ is not the lifeless harmless image he has hitherto been to you, but a rallying centre for revolutionary influences . . . , you must look to yourselves; for you have brought the image to life; and the mob may not be able to bear that horror." [4]

The crowd offers its acclaim on the condition that it can claim Christ for its own; Christ claims the crowd for God. So long as men can read their images and desires into Christ, they are well content. But when he cracks through their ironclad minds and makes his larger meaning perfectly plain—that he intends to lead them beyond the boundaries of self to God—many draw back not because they do not understand, but because they do. Here endeth the joy ride and here beginneth the joyless broken-hearted, rather than broken-imaged flight.

[4] George Bernard Shaw, *Androcles and the Lion,* preface (New York: Brentano's, 1916). By permissions of The Public Trustee and the Society of Authors.

Very close to refusal through conditional acceptance is refusal through *partial acceptance*. Here the condition is that discipleship shall be confined to strata—often to as little as one more or less unimportant segment—of horizontal experience and shall not be permitted to become the dimension of height and depth through the whole. This technique is analagous to the preservation of national sovereignty through a truce which grants concessions of inconsequential territories, petty tribute, and token fealties. "You want to be king?" "Yea, Lord, I surrender to you the domain of Ten Percent, yours to hold in sway to perpetuity. No doubt I can expect your governance to multiply prosperity within this adjacent region, so that increased trade will indirectly benefit my holdings. But look you stay within your own borders and encroach not upon my territory where I am monarch!" This may be the technique of the rich young ruler and all those who are not far from the kingdom of God. Implicit in it is that the man shall remain divided against himself.

A particularly insidious form of partial acceptance which ought to be mentioned is *emotional refusal*. Thus one goes to the gospel feast, but retains the emotional bias which separates him from his fellow guests. Or what is equally common, one accepts Christ emotionally but in no other way. The stigmata in Jesus' hands and feet and side were not emotionally induced. They were actual.

The attempt to break down the structure of decision at the point of time is *refusal by procrastination*. By putting acceptance off to the future one hopes to ignore the fact that it has meant refusal in the present. "I will follow you; Lord; but let me first . . . ." (Luke 9:61.)

What is not always so sharply brought into focus is the

fact that procrastination has a reverse gear, too. The decision may be as dangerously put off into the past as put off into the future. This is evasion of the "now" factor by saying, "I *have* done it; I need not do it *now*." This fugitive will fly him "down the arches of years" that have been. It will be impossible for millions to respond to the Christian invitation until they have first rid themselves of the illusion that they already have.

This very delusion of having secured the faith as a once-for-all possession is itself proof of its loss. When we imagine that accepting Christ's invitation is something that we have done and have done with, either we did not at the beginning understand the nature of it as something the ever-active God does about which we must do something, or else "on the way we lost it." The most likely place we lost it was in a rut.

When retrograde procrastination has petrified, we sometimes call it "habit"—"sometimes," because in fairness we must distinguish (even though by doing it we leave a loophole and even though we know that for the fugitive every loophole is a "leap hole") between habit, which is slavery to routine, and custom or tradition, which is free loyalty to and appropriation of a heritage. In the kingdom of God, there is no such thing as a good habit. Heaven has no habits at all. Habit is a deep, dividing chasm which cuts man off from the kingdom. It is behavior in a rut and a rut, we hear it said, "is a grave with the ends knocked out." I am confident this is that selfsame ditch by which Jesus saw the two blind men imperiled.

At best, habit is decision which has died and been buried in the spinal column. More often it is not even the mummy of one's own decision but "playing dead" like a dog someone else has trained. Habit is a technique of self-slavery, and like all slavery it seems convenient; but the self is created for freedom before God. It is just this self-perpetuating behavior which needs to be jolted to a halt so that society may cease its lemming-like surge toward suicide and come under the control of man. No matter at how much pain decision first was made, nor with what care it was etched, entrenched, entombed, and engraved in the ganglia, the habit is a gilded cage: no matter how good of its kind, its kind is bad. No more than those stamped into conformity by "the religion of the social routine," right actions performed under the duress of conditioned response, although they may result in respectability, do not constitute faith. Discipleship degenerated to habit is no decision.

Behold a dilemma: habit is decision's shadow. We are always in danger of keeping the shadow and not the substance, the form and not the power of religion. In this sense the evangelist does great wrong ever to talk about "cultivating holy habits of the Christian life"—disciplines, yes; habits, no. For the moment Christianity becomes habitual it ceases to be holy, ceases to be Christianity, and becomes but another graven image. It does not then produce men who have been raised from death to life: it merely transfers the corpse to a grave in sanctified soil.

We dare not urge people to make a habit of Christ (oh, what a thought!), but always to make a decision for Christ. No, we dare not even make or urge others to make a habit of making the decision. Thus, in responding habitually to Christ's call, we do not really respond to him who calls but to the habit. It is like letting someone else bear the responsibility for decision. Habit, *involuntary acceptance*, destroys decision at the crucial point of will operating in freedom. Habitual piety is decision's death mask. Woe to the evangelist who suffocates souls with it.

The fossilized decision of the past is seldom adequate to meet the challenge of the present, for "time makes ancient good uncouth." My habitual patterns of response to Christ, formed from what were, in the past, true adventures in faith, may lead me to betray Christ in the present situation. My stereotyped image of a past decision may prevent me from recognizing and following the surging contemporary Christ.

The writer of Genesis figured the tempter as a serpent as subtle as he is supple. It should be clear that we have by no means exhausted all the possible methods of refusal, nor have we mapped all the serpentine slithering of which a man is capable as he flees from God down the dark labyrinthine ways of his own mind; and it is equally plain that men are fully able to improvise fiendish combinations of several methods. Such attempts to break through the walls of the decision-structure as we have catalogued them here commend themselves to the fugitive as deceptive means by which he can appear to follow while in reality he flies— means by which he can appear to have his apple while in reality he eats it, means by which he can appear to deny the nature of the forced option with which Christ confronts him. Yet if and when all these attempts have been uncovered, even when the masquerade of innocence is ripped away, refusal is still possible. The decision can be "No."

These variations are only methods. Now let us turn to examine the reasons, whether they be stated or implied, for which the methods are used.

7

REASONS FOR REFUSAL

Meet a man with a new leash on life: "I have married a wife, and therefore I cannot come" (Luke 14:20).

This is at least a refreshing change from today's popular dodge: "Of course we're with you; I'll be represented by my wife!" But in addition to the man who believes in God as his heavenly Father-in-law, we still encounter some who say, "I will come when my wife comes," and so permit the human relationship to undercut the divine relationship on which it is based.

In Jesus' story, the two other intended guests also sent their regrets: "They all alike ["with one consent"—K.J.V.] began to make excuses. . . . 'I have bought a field, and I must go and see it; I pray you, have me excused.' . . . . 'I have bought five yoke of oxen, and I go to examine them; I pray you, have me excused'" (Luke 14:18-19). Each is saying in effect, "I believe my welfare is best served by pursuing these goals." A solid case can be presented to show that their objectives also minister to the welfare of the entire community. Family, property, work—all represent fulfilled possibilities. Conversely, each concrete freedom has mean the abandonment of other castles in Spain. Our problem is to have nothing in such a way that keeps the best from having us.

These three men show no desire to be rude to the host. They seem to have nothing against him personally; neither do they love him so intensely that they will surrender their own projects to come to his party. They will send their regrets, but they do not regret it enough to come. It is "No" wrapped in a pink ribbon: "I pray you, have me excused. . . . I cannot come."

To treat as of first and ultimate concern—that is, what we shall call "to absolutize"—the pursuit of anything less than God is idolatry. Princeton professor Emile Cailliet has discerned that the unholy trinity is made up of these idols: Baal, Moloch, and Mammon.[1] The three abstaining guests in Jesus' parable may be taken as devotees of the cults of these.

Baal is the god of physical life and fertility. His—or her—ritual is sexual: not only sexual, but basically. Baalism is the unwarranted conclusion that the physical means of life are not only the reason how but the reason why, the purpose of life. The aim of Baalism is to achieve at-one-ment with the natural forces upon which natural life is dependent. In addition to self-enjoyment, self-preservation, and self-perpetuation, the worshiper is offered the sense that although he is finally destroyed by these same natural forces, he is then assimilated again into the tomb—or womb—of mother earth from which he sprang: "The sum of man . . . to revel and to rot." This nature-god is securely ensconced in mankind's pantheon. What student of anthropology,

[1] Emile Cailliet, *The Dawn of Personality* (Indianapolis and New York: The Bobbs-Merrill Company, 1955), p. 136.

of history, of philosophy, of psychology, of literature, of religion, does not know of Baal and his numerous court, not to mention courtesans? Who has not been awed by his appearance, swayed by his power? Baal is still in business.

Waltz of the Toreadors, by outstanding existentialist dramatist Jean Anouilh, toured America under the advertisement "Sex Farce," an ironically appropriate billing since one may read the play's message as saying that life consisting only of sex is indeed a farce! General St. Pé, grown old and bitter from having gone through the motions but not the emotions of marriage, is expounding his lack-lusty philosophy of life to his secretary, a pure and earnest young man named Gaston:

General: The ideal, my friend, is the lifebuoy. You're in the ocean, splashing about, doing your damndest not to drown, in spite of whirlpools and cross currents. The main thing is to do the regulation breast-stroke and if you're not a clod, never to let the lifebuoy out of your sight. No one expects any more than that of you. If you relieve yourself in the water now and then, that's your affair. The sea is big, and if the top half of your body still looks as though it's doing the regulation breast-stroke, nobody will say a word.

Secretary: But does one never reach the lifebuoy, General?

General: Never. But if your heart's in the right place, you never lose sight of it either. Fanatics who try a faster stroke to reach it at all costs, deluge everybody else and always finish up by drowning, generally dragging God knows how many poor devils under with them, who could otherwise have gone on quietly floundering about and minding their own business.

At this moment—the peak theatrical moment in the production—a woman two seats over from me announced audibly and fervently, "I agree with him!" With equal gusto the woman who was my immediate neighbor responded, "Me, too!" The girls had stuck their necks out. They forgot that the French have a reputation for handling the guillotine, and now the blade came flashing:

Secretary: Might I say something, though?

General: Go ahead, my boy. Your turn to speak now.

Secretary: I am twenty years old, General. I would rather try to go fast and drown.

General: (Gently, after a pause.) You are right, my boy. It's a sorry business, growing old, and understanding. (In a sudden cry.) Lieutenant St. Pé! Graduated second from Saumur! Volunteer! Wait for me! I'm done for anyway—here goes, I'd rather drown!

Were my theater neighbors unusual, or will you find many to agree with them—keep up surface appearance a bit and wallow all you will? In fact, will you find some who deliberately plash about in the soup in an effort to escape the necessity placed upon them by the gracious goal of life? But over the waves the light can be seen and no darkness can shut it out. It is another Frenchman who has given us the tale of a gentleman who is crowned with a radiant halo. His wife finds it a social liability, so to oblige her he attempts to get rid of it, preparing for lust by reading sex manuals aloud. But at the end of the story, even as a purveyor, his head is still ringed with the glowing

[2] From *Waltz of the Toreadors* by Jean Anouilh; tr. by Lucienne Hill. By permission of Dr. Jan Van Loewen, Ltd.

nimbus.[3] The man sought by God is a marked man; and though he plunge into the depths of a sea of sensuality, he has not escaped the gracious calling of the Lord.

The Cult of Carnality is elaborated to include much more than just sex for self-perpetuation and self-enjoyment, though that element remains persistent in it. In its more sophisticated forms, Baalism embraces the most of scientism and materialism, systems which deceptively appear to demand of the adherent neither faith nor sacrifice and in which the how and why of life are determined and explained by reference to "nature."

When the evangelist seeks to persuade by offering to put into the control of his converts magically operative laws and forces by means of which they may escape their anxious creatureliness and have animal contentments without man's essential tensions, he may well ask himself whether he is not more truly proselytizing in behalf of Baal.

The Cult of Cruelty is composed of the worshipers of *Moloch*. The ethic of these is to sacrifice others to achieve one's own ends. The Moloch-iavellian aims at self-assertion: "They have but one law, to seize the power and keep it." [4] If we were defining the term more precisely, we should have to say that they aim at that power called "force," which in the eyes of the Christian is a substitute for—the tacit admission of the absence of—real power, particularly the power to be and to be free. The invited guest who preferred to road test his oxen was looking after his private power supply. He was surely no high priest of Moloch; he

[3] Marcel Aymé, *Across Paris and Other Stories* (New York: Harper & Brothers, 1958), pp. 95 ff.

[4] From *Murder in the Cathedral* by T.S. Eliot, copyright, 1935, by Harcourt, Brace and Company, Inc., and by Faber and Faber Ltd.

was simply a man who was more interested in seeing raw force harnessed for his own ends than he was in directing himself to the feast.

Moloch's cult possibly originated as a religion of nationalism, and we see it recrudescent in all nationalistic power lust. "I have made a new bomb, and I go to test it. I have developed a new missile, and I go to test it"—Moloch's devotees are more excited by the means of death than by the means of life. When nations or men trust force, they act as if Moloch were God—or as if God were Moloch. In the thirteenth century, to choose a safe distance, Martino de Canale recorded such a case of mistaken identity:

> Now would I . . . that every one and all know forever the works of the Venetians. . . . How they are all perfect in the faith of Jesu Christ and obedient to holy Church. . . . Within this noble Venice there dares to dwell neither heretic, nor usurer, murderer, thief nor robber. . . . And I will tell you the names of the noble captains whom the noble Doges sent in their time to lay low their enemies.[5]

Every man who stands more in awe of unleashed force than of the spirit which directs force to minister to life pays obeisance to Moloch. Every man who individually or corporately looks on another human being as a rung in a ladder and the instrument of his desires participates in the ancient blood ritual. Teaching of self-sacrifice for Christ's sake, if perverted to a demand that someone else sacrifice himself or his goods for my sake, has become the worship of Moloch. Few attractions are more forceful than

---

[5] Quoted in Eileen Power, *Medieval People* (Boston: Houghton Mifflin Co., 1924), p. 29.

the promise of power, and the evangelist is beset with temptation at this point. Indeed, Christian evangelism is used as a technique for recruitment to the cults of Moloch and his fellows when faith in Christ is urged for the sake of preserving the strength and supremacy of a nation against the force of a "godless" enemy, or whenever an evangelist considers converts as the means to accomplish his own aims.

Mammonism, the Cult of Covetousness, aims at self-aggrandizement. Whereas Baalism measures its brand of holiness in amount of pleasure and the worship of Moloch measures by the extent of power, Mammonism measures success in terms of possessions: "The god is profits, and opportunism the ritual of worship." [6] "I have bought a field." No reason for refusal does Jesus attack more determinedly than this, no obstacle in the path of man does he consider more serious. "A man's life does not consist in the abundance of his possessions." (Luke 12:15.) How hard for a rich man to enter the kingdom! If camels cannot pass through the needle's eye, how shall a man squeeze a two-garage car through the strait and narrow gate?

Again the division we have been using is largely artificial—how else describe artifice? It is obvious that the three—Baal, Moloch and Mammon—are an unholy trinity, ever one idol. We have been employing the three impersonations as transparent objectifications for what are commonly called "motives": pleasure, power and profit motives. It will be our argument that these are not true motives at all, but that each idol represents one mode in which the basic motive makes itself manifest.

[6] Hortense Powdermaker, *Hollywood: The Dream Factory* (Boston: Little, Brown and Company, 1950), p. 108.

For the moment, we observe that the idols are in fact inseparable. For example, both Moloch and Mammon may presuppose the reality of Baal. The man who, at the cost of his soul, forcibly steals another man's bread or raises ever more storehouses for his grain may be acting on the assumption that man shall live by bread alone. Again, both Moloch and Mammon may be Baal's servants, so that one man might hope to find pleasure in or through power or possession, while another may fancy that if he has possessions he will be guaranteed either pleasure or power, or both. Or sex and possessions may be made instruments of cruelty. There is scarcely an end to the nefarious teamwork of the infernal triangle. But the result of their co-operation is always the same—to devour their worshiper. They pull against one another to tear him apart. Thus, a man desiring the pleasure of affection while at the same time indulging a need to dominate others is torn asunder between the clutches of Baal and Moloch.

Moreover, our understanding of the worship of the unholy three—mistaking the means of life for the meaning of life—must include their kingdoms, all the specific systems developed for the manipulation of the idols: social systems for Baal, political systems for Moloch, and economic systems for Mammon. The idols' influence pervades every area of experience through the often interchangeable elements of these systems such as art, literature, science, institutionalized religion, education, government, and entertainment. As inside one man, theirs is still a conspiracy for conflict, so that one historian can contend, for example, that the chief objectives of American life are "the desire to see all men free and equal, and the desire to be richer and stronger than anyone else." [7] A nation in the grip of idols may desire to be well thought of by all other nations and to perpetuate its own existence, while at the same time it boasts of the superior abundance of its possessions and advertises its capacity to destroy any other nation.

Whether it be a nation or a man, the call of Christ appears at the first to add one more conflict. He does not peacefully join the assassins' conspiracy but brings against them a sword.

Still using the labels transparently, this trinity helps expose the classic New Testament refusal of Christ's invitation when the rich young ruler turned his back on life. He gets his composite name from the three synoptics, but we may take each name to represent one idol and we may take the composite to represent any person with a future before him, with some influence somewhere, whose ascendant identification is through possessions. The man need not actually have all or any of these three; all that is necessary to fill our requirements is that he have a compulsion towards them.

I have met the rich young ruler several times and have never failed to be struck by his likeness to myself. On one occasion an every member canvass worker reported to the campaign chairman that he had made a disastrous call on some newly transferred members who had promised him they would never again burden the pews of our church. Since I have a morbid curiosity about making autopsies on dissatisfied constituents, I visited the head of that household to see what holes in our net needed mending.

He was a personable young man with a lovely family.

---

[7] Roger Butterfield, *The American Past: A History of the United States from Concord to Hiroshima* (New York: Simon & Schuster, 1947), p. 5.

It seemed almost a shame to dissect; however, I began the probe carefully, layer by layer, to get through the superficial to the heart. The preliminary anesthetic which he administered to me was that I should understand he held no malice against me as man or minister; the anesthetic he gave himself was to assure me and himself that the religious life was of deep concern to him. Then commenced the indictment: (a) He, nor his children, cared for our Sunday-school facilities. (*I reminded him that at that moment a new building was being erected.*) (b) At first his children had cried in their classes. (*They no longer did, he admitted.*) (c) Well, to speak the damaging truth, he just did not like my preaching. (*And I, looking on him, loathed him.*) He wanted the preacher to tell him he was a sinner "and if I don't repent I'm going to hell." (*Wishing to justify myself, I opined that if he were an unrepentant sinner there was no chance of him going to hell; he was already there. I followed up this tactful thrust with a deep breath to get myself in hand to continue the exploration. I knew my preaching could not be at the bottom of it! At last we reached what my outraged vanity was relieved to consider the root of the matter. This was the clincher—and come to think of it, my sermons certainly were at default*). (d) "And I just don't like this Every Member Canvass. I don't stand still for anyone telling me what to give!"

Those, dear heart, are the rich young ruler's very words: "I don't stand still for anyone telling me what to give!" Respectability is a cinch, righteousness is a snap, confession is easy, but to make a change in one's life . . . !

I went away maliciously satisfied that I had been unjustly booted because I happened to stand between the mule and the intended target—and by my concern for self-exoneration showing how justly I deserved to be booted—profoundly dissatisfied that in all of our subsequent conversation I was unable to persuade this fine young man that discipleship means stewardship.

The New Testament's rich young ruler, who, when you consider the characteristics implied by those words, was neither rich, young, nor ruler, went away sorrowful. Send his regrets? He kept them.

Without doubt the gospel writers are correct to single out Mammon as the idol who tripped up the rich young ruler. But Jesus' further invitation to "come, follow me," would have rubbed henchmen Baal and Moloch the wrong way, too. The "ruler" would have had to become a follower, the "youth," an eternity older, if not a corpse on a cross. All three points, meant to be hinges on which the door to life swings, became bolts to shut Jesus out.

We have looked at some of the methods of evasion. We have asked the question, "Why do we evade?" and found the answer, "Because we are idolaters and follow after Baal, Moloch, and Mammon." These are the elemental spirits, the principalities and powers against which the evangelist must wrestle. These are the idols from whom he must woo invited guests. To do it he must understand that the real issue is not idols; it is idolatry. He must know why man is an idolater, what the weakness is in man that gives these "gods that are no gods" their grip on his affections, their attraction, their power to destroy him. To heal, the evangelist must find the flaw in the heart of man where idols breed.

8

THE CAUSE OF REFUSAL

Sin is separation. The root cause for refusal of the reconciling invitation, and the source of idolatry, is man's attempt to establish his identity independently from God.[1] The function and the attraction of idols are to provide man some tolerable answer to the question "Who am I?" Man follows false gods who promise protection from what he fears is the destructive truth about himself—that he is insignificant, helpless, alone in a hostile universe, and guilty before God. But in lending man an alias, the idols give him the truly disastrous illusion of having an acceptable self.

To understand the way in which this false identity may be assumed it is only necessary to remind ourselves that what a man seeks determines what a man is, and then to observe the important corollary: the standard of measurement by which a man chooses to be judged has the same effect of determining what that man is. This is so because each criterion has its appropriate goal, each act of worship its appropriate object.

One who measures man by money has absolutized Mam-

[1] Gilkey, *op. cit.*, p. 195.

mon. Confronted with an example such as Rembrandt—
who lived much of his life in poverty and finally died
destitute, but for all that could hardly be counted a man
worth nothing—the Mammonite will blandly reply "Ah,
but today his paintings are worth a fortune!" By judging
the man Rembrandt in terms of picture price tags, he
has demonstrated his assumption that Rembrandt's essential
purpose or value can be—and should be—expressed in
monetary symbols and therefore is monetary. If another
considers Rembrandt a "good" man because he is a good
artist, he may be assuming that the purpose, and conse-
quently the value, of the man Rembrandt lies in artistic
ability. This might be a different thing from contending
that by impressing meaningful form on material Rembrandt has expressed a spiritual quality which glorifies God
the creator. Just as the one who applies as an absolute the
measure of money thereby implies that man's purpose is to
win a crown of gold, so also those who apply as absolutes
the measures of pleasure or force thereby imply that the
aim of man is to achieve satisfaction or to dominate. Since
the measurement employed points to a goal and since a man
is what he follows, we must agree with Kierkegaard that
a thing or a person qualitatively is what it is measured by,
at least to the person accepting the measurement as valid.

The man who says, "My goal is to glorify God" and
who then proceeds to measure himself by the barns he
builds for his own ease deceives himself. The greater importance of this corollary that a measurement implies a
definition lies in the fact that while few men openly declare
for demonic ends as such, and many never consciously
declare for any goal at all, almost all men do use some

standard of self-measurement and thus unwittingly commit and define themselves.

A typical example of this pattern of idolatry by acceptance of an idol's rule may be found in the New Testament in the picture of the chief tax collector, Zacchaeus. (Luke 19:1-10.) "He was small of stature," the plight of every man in the universe. A short man wearing psychological elevator shoes, Zacchaeus tried to make himself appear taller by standing on a pile of money he earned doing the Romans' tax collecting—a sure method for winning the heartfelt hatred of his people. Thus his need for a standing with his fellows drove him to try to gain it by means which could, in reality, accomplish nothing but alienation.

The normal and powerful drive of compensation in order to gain acceptability may propel men to heights—and it may also destroy their freedom of self-determination, their happiness, their selves. Not all bald men are Caesars, not all short men are Napoleons. We used to tell about the stutterer who, like Demosthenes, for ten years practiced speaking with pebbles in his mouth. Crowds at last gathered to hear him speak and they all went away exclaiming, "He sounds like he's got a mouthful of pebbles!"

Mere possession of a defect is no guarantee of going far, and falling short of the glory of God is no guarantee of attaining salvation. Consciousness of being cut off from others by failure to attain an acceptable identity may simply increase envy and anxiety and spur a man on to mount the treacherous ladder of that form of ambition by which many men have climbed and "step by step . . . ascended into Hell."

Depth indicators of descent into idolatry—outward and visible signs of inferior and mistaken standards—are embodied in evanescent symbols which we may call "trophies." A catalogue of these proofs of piety would have to include the traditional loving cups (now there is a trophy name to conjure with!) and framed documents, automobiles, boats, homes, executive suites, fashionable uniforms, occasionally a spouse, company kept, social events attended, job held, and various patterns of behavior, to name but a few. In preference to long robes, the trophy may be verbal— "Rabbi! Rabbi!"—and a title attached like a dog tag to a name. However diverse, all the trophies may be used as convenient index numbers to establish an identity. The status seekers are identity seekers. The trophies, the titles, the marks of prestige—all set that person apart from others. But the life which is measured by externals—by "things of the flesh"—is external, is flesh. Since the external is the obvious, it is the standard most easily and therefore most often accepted by men. Few, like Cyrano de Bergerac, are content to wear, or are even mildly interested in wearing, their adornments on their souls because the entire purpose of idolatry is to be identified by men and not to be identified by God. In a world blinded by sights, provided I can "make a good showing in the flesh," provided only I have a trophy, the spiritual may atrophy and it does not matter at all, it is not noticed at all.

Our national obsession with such trophies, our incessant competition to be big men on a small scale, "superior specimens of an inferior type," indicate our thorough commitment to the value scales of finite goals, that is, to the worship of idols. And when we reflect on the social derivation of many of these scales of value and remember how often the assent they are given is unconscious or how often they are passively accepted as "the rules of the game," we are again reminded that to practice an evangelism which is only individualistic is like telling a typhoid patient he must drink pure water while leaving the only well in the oasis polluted. Society itself may be idolatrous, and man cannot live apart from society.

Zacchaeus was in society but not in community. Those who let his sense of inferiority or his collaborationism shut him out of their circles did so in the name of their own restrictive idols as well as his. How many who did not hate him on account of his bid for wealth and recognition ridiculed him for it? Behind the clownish figure he cut—a little man, heavy-laden with the rings and robes of brief authority, trying to strut—who had the heart to see a suffering man who feared or hated or envied a world to which he could not belong?

The whole operation of idolatry, we now see, is directed not really toward the idol, which is by definition not ultimate, but away from our fellows. If the idol were ultimate and its scale of measurement therefore infinite, then it would follow that every point on that scale would be equally—that is, infinitely—distant from the goal. And each person, no matter where he chanced to fall on that scale, would fall infinitely short of the goal. Therefore, from the point of view of an infinitely distant goal, all would have the same status. So idolaters measure themselves not in relation to an ultimate goal but by comparing their position with that of other persons. The idea of a scale is the idea of difference or distance. Thus idolatry is inherently invidious, and so the very act of attempting to join others on these terms is the occasion of alienation from them—which is only to be expected when we have defined sin as separation. As Zacchaeus may have learned by bitter lesson, this attitude can infect even—or especially—religion and produce pharisaism. "But when they measure themselves by one another, and compare themselves with one another, they are without understanding." (II Cor. 10: 12*b*.) What man needs is a God, to draw near whom is to draw near his fellows.

Another result of the fact that, even though treated as absolute, idols are relative is that idolatry fails to master anxiety. As well as anxiety about position there is anxiety about permanence. All of our identification by medals is the substitution of symbols for a self. But the question "Who am I?" is an ultimate question, and anything less than an ultimate answer fails to satisfy. Though I win laurel wreaths and victors' crowns, anxiety remains:

> . . . for within the hollow crown
> That rounds the mortal temples of a king
> Keeps Death his court and there the antick sits,
> Scoffing his state and grinning at his pomp,
> Allowing him a breath, a little scene,
> To monarchize, be fear'd, and kill with looks,
> Infusing him with self and vain conceit
> As if this flesh which walls about our life,
> Were brass impregnable; and humor'd thus
> Comes at the last and with a little pin
> Bores through his castle wall, and farewell, king! [2]

But impermanence of possession does nothing to loosen my death-grip on straws. With no identity in eternity, a final, lastingly futile trophy will be raised—my headstone.

When we measure ourselves by trick rulers we deceive

[2] *King Richard II*, Act iii, sc. 2.

ourselves and as many others as accept our standards of measurement. Yet the deception, at the points of alienation and the anxiety it nourishes while it hides, is a fragile façade and must be supported by main force. We may not even choose to support it, but it protects us—the standards we have constitute all the life we have—and all our energy must be thrown desperately into shoring it up. If our trophies are gone, we are gone; should anyone ring the bell on our false scales of value, we are finished. No wonder one anthropologist can observe that some Americans "give the impression of Cinderella at the ball, just before the clock strikes midnight." [3] Jesus rings the bell.

Zacchaeus, "short of stature," met the measure of the stature of the mature man in Jesus. Christ is God's standard for all men's lives. Man is invited to measure himself, his possessions, his achievements, and his affections by the immeasureable infinite Spirit of God. In the sense of measurement of which we have been speaking, this is impossible. Just so.

A man accepting this new measurement exists in a new way with respect to God and not man. Relative and invidious comparisons are destroyed; the familiar pharisaic slogan "I am no worse than," or, "I am as good as others" is obliterated in the challenge: "Be perfect, as God is perfect"—the point of that command to perfection consisting in its utter impossibility which makes an absurdity of all comparison with other men or measurement by externals. All have fallen infinitely short of that glory; pride cannot feed on this food. Thus, belief that God is wholly other is the very belief which makes reconcilation

[3] Powdermaker, *op. cit.*, p. 37.

possible. "That which is born of the flesh is flesh, and that which is born of the Spirit is Spirit" (John 3:6). This new conception is the new birth and the new life. Measured by Spirit, man now is Spirit.

By the same token, let a man accept the measurement of Spirit, and although he were the "least" servant in the household of the Lord—if such were true—he would have become infinitely "greater" than any king of the world of externals. For as his measure is infinitely greater, so is his goal; and therefore, so is he. In the realm of the finite, desire is insatiable; in the realm of the infinite, fulfillment is inexhaustible.

Zacchaeus accepted Christ joyfully. But not all do.

King Harry I of Harrisonia wrote an ultimatum to the president of the United States. The president must recognize the new nation of Harrisonia or else "reason with a .22 Winchester."

"King Harry" was a twelve-year-old boy who liked to send away box tops. His threatening letter was one of many turned over to the Secret Service for investigation in 1956. To the House Appropriations Committee, the Secret Service Chief reported:

Investigation disclosed that a breakfast cereal company distributes deeds to a square inch of land in Alaska to persons sending in the used box top, and Harry and several of his playmates received deeds from the company.

Harry . . . and his playmates decided to band together, form their own country, and secede from the union.

There was no prosecution in this case, and the boy's mother agreed a severe lecture was in order. The boy was normal but had an overactive imagination.

He did not realize the seriousness of his threat against the

President, and when the possible consequences were explained to him, he replied, "I surrender. I am now a citizen again."

On the human side, King Harry's misadventure is the accurate analogy of man's rebellion. He seeks a crown but does not know the way to get it. It is one thing for an imaginative boy to play King Harry; it is another for a man in the vain imaginings of his heart to play King Herod. Yet it comes even to that when man stakes his absolute claim to his square inch and asserts his independence from the very ground of his existence. Then his behavior, fatally logical from its false presumption, may exhibit all the symptoms of insanity, leaving him totally divorced from his real situation and completely mistaking his identity. Having made his "heaven to dream upon a crown," he considers as his enemy anyone who would tell him the truth. Let an ambassador be sent to plead with him and, as we have seen, no evasion seems too absurd for him to attempt. To maintain unbroken his dream of kingship he will:

> Deceive more slily than Ulysses could,
> And, like a Sinon, take another Troy.
> [He] can add colours to the chameleon,
> Change shapes with Proteus for advantages,
> And set the murderous Machiavel to school.[4]

On communication from the King he may only pretend to accept the message; he may offer a provisional treaty; he may attempt to bribe with nonessential concessions. But if these dodges are thwarted, he may begin to "hew [his]

[4] *III Henry VI*, Act iii, sc. 2.

way out with a bloody axe": beat one messenger, kill another, stone the next. He may come at length to the depth of dissociation, and when the princely Son is sent, say, "This is the heir; come, let us kill him, and the inheritance will be ours" (Mark 12:7). O irony! when the Prince has come to make him brother and joint heir.

Man clings to his idols for the illusion of an acceptable self which they give him, and he refuses to answer the calling of Christ or to discover the truth which is in Christ, because he is afraid that the truth for him, as it did for Oedipus the king, means disaster. He sees the gift of God as the destruction of the external life he has and not as the birth of a new life in the Spirit. He is afraid to be known by his name instead of his aliases, afraid to take his place before God instead of the place he can have before men, afraid to gauge his standing by faith instead of evidences, because he is afraid to see himself as a sinner. He prefers the masquerade he can present to men and refuses to see himself as he appears to God. He will not turn aside from his idols' macabre cortege to join in the wedding procession because he fears that his death mask will be smashed and underneath shall be found dead man's bones.

But what if God does not despise the humble and contrite heart? What if the sinner is not left alone and separated, but God is with him? And what if to draw close to him who in Christ has drawn close to man is to draw close to all men? What if man is not helpless but upheld by the hand of God? What if the truth in Christ about man is that man is not insignificant but precious, endowed by God with the value of sacrificial love? If I, a sinner, should somehow become convinced that this is the true relationship between a sinner and his God, that this is the truth, that this is the ultimate answer to the question of my identity, I would smash my hideous idols, run, cast my trophies at his feet, crown him Lord of all, and from his hand receive with joy a crown of life.

The story is told that when, during World War I, the emperor of Austria-Hungary died after having ruled for more than sixty years, he was carried as his fathers before him were to the crypt of the Church of the Capuchins in Vienna. When the escort knocked at the gate a voice from inside offered the traditional challenge: "Who is there?" The reply: "His Serene Majesty, the Emperor of Austria." The graveside liturgist sang: "I know him not. Who is there?" Again the answer: "The Apostolic King of Hungary." But once more the voice demanded: "I know him not. Who is there?" This time the suppliant's answer was: "Our brother Franz Josef, a sinner." At that, the gates opened and the emperor was admitted to rest among his ancestors.

The gates to human and divine fellowship, the gates to the kingdom, the door of life, open to that name.

PART
FOUR

ACCEPTANCE

9

THE MEANS OF ACCEPTANCE

Since we have seen that all the evasions and all the re-
fusals are symptoms of idolatry, it would therefore appear
that when this has been revealed, the self would gladly
depose and discard its treacherous gods. But this is as
likely as blithely suggesting to a condemned prisoner that
he ought to leave death row. We have observed that
idolatry (wrong trust) is in turn a symptom of sin (wrong
love), and that idolatry's function is to offer the self protection from the truth. Moreover, this false sense of self-
security can also be fed by some pious-sounding jargon
like, "What you don't know won't hurt you." This false
sense of security lends the self illusions of power, pleasure,
and possession—yet this victim of idolatry never sees ultimate power—only finite. His idolatrous worship removes
him from any satisfaction in fellowship—as a matter of
fact his greatest fears are of other people, and of death.
Man's attempts to engineer his own escape from these fears
only compound his idolatry and reassert his sin. No, although idols betray, freedom from bondage to their forces

of sin and death is not in the power of man. He needs ultimates and infinites, not finites!

Then by what means can a man accept Christ's standard of the infinite Spirit of God, and with it, his new life in the Spirit? How is one enabled to forsake his assumed identity before God? For that matter, if life according to the flesh is inevitably divisive, then does not invidiousness to the nth degree inhere much more in this measurement of man—finite fallen creature—by the Spirit of God, wholly other creator of heaven and earth?

Yes, it is possible that the very means of salvation, the revelation of God in Christ, may be so perverted by a man's misunderstanding or an evangelist's presentation that it does not bridge but widens the chasm. Let a man do nothing more than measure himself by Christ, and the result will be despair; and as we have seen, it is this which sends men scurrying. The winsomeness of Jesus does not lie in the perfection of his manhood but in the perfection of his love. The work of an evangelist is therefore to lead a man to the place where he is able to accept Christ's measure because he has accepted Christ's love. Without that good news, Christ is bad news.

A man finds it to be an actual impossibility to measure up to the stature of Christ. Heroic effort on heroic effort results in failure on failure until the inevitable happens: one is driven from the impossible to the possible, from God to idols, from Christ to man, from Spirit to trophies. In his despair this man—and often he is the man in our churches, not to say in our pulpits—turns his frustration and self-contempt on others in order to soothe the sting of his defeat, to draw attention from his inward separation, and to cover up his sense of guilt by making others appear inferior, and therefore more guilty. He becomes caught in this whirl-pool. The perfection of Christ has driven him to spotlight, to magnify—yes, even to create—imperfections in his fellows. Frustrated, he seeks to frustrate others; powerless to free himself, he seeks the sensation of power by crushing others. Unable to add one cubit to his own stature, he seeks the illusion of growth by cutting others down to his size—and smaller.

But how does this differ from a parasitic existence, sustained by feeding on the lives of others? It does not differ. This man, having begun with the Spirit and ended with the flesh, is the same old "natural" man who has no life of his own, but lives a vampire life through exploitation. As Pascal saw:

Man would fain be great and sees that he is little; would fain be happy and sees that he is miserable; would fain be perfect and sees that he is full of imperfections; would fain be the object of the love and esteem of men, and sees that his faults merit only their aversion and contempt. The embarrassment wherein he finds himself produces in him the most unjust and criminal passions imaginable, for he conceives a mortal hatred against that truth which blames him and convinces him of his faults.[1]

Of course it is disguised with acceptable names, such as "love" and "sacrifice." But beneath the sounds and tinkling syllables we see the mother who devours her child's life by overprotection, the man who donates to the church in order to buy his way, and all those others with whom love is a vulture because the coming of the perfect, rather than doing away with, has by contrast emphasized their own

[1] Pascal, *Pensées*.

imperfections. To such as these, the perfection of Christ has not been understood as perfect love.

Therefore it is essential that the evangelist himself constantly experience the love of Christ, else his evangelism may be not God's love for sinners but envy's denunciation of fools. Negative preaching, a mantle of threadbare moral indignation cloaking filthy rags, a patronizing attitude of spiritual superiority—anything and everything that is called evangelism but is in reality only recrimination, the spouting of a guilt complex so high-pressured it has burst its pipes, may have more the effect of a death warrant than an invitation to life. Such "evangelism" may itself agitate the vortex and draw men deeper into idolatry.

Christianity has said that the perfection of love—the character of God—is perfectly revealed in the Cross: "God shows his love for us in that while we were yet sinners Christ died for us" (Rom. 5:8). If Christ's cross is to be for us anything more than the supreme indictment of the human race, if instead of plunging man further into despair and hostility, the Cross is to save, then we must see on Calvary—and the evangelist must help us to see—not only the conviction of our sin but also what Victor Hugo called the "supreme happiness of life . . . the conviction that we are loved," loved perfectly, loved ultimately, loved seriously by God. If either is to be understood, the Cross must reveal to us at once the depth of sin and the height of love.

But let the evangelist be warned that by leading the lost to the Cross and saying, "See the sin of man and the love of God; how God's love has overcome man's sin. Will you not live for him who died for you?" he has brought his friend to just that point which most repels, for the love which man needs above all things is above all things hard to accept. If it were something he could win; but to accept! The idea that Christ shall take my place, that I shall receive his inheritance as his free gift, that the judge who declares me guilty at the same moment removes my guilt—all this seems an outrageous insult. I demand the right to what I deserve. That is, I demand treatment as an independent being. Even though it would mean death, at least the death would be mine, and that would establish my separate identity. But if Christ has made the "full, perfect, and sufficient sacrifice, oblation, and satisfaction, for the sins of the whole world," then I am not to be accorded even the wry solace of paying my own debts or going bankrupt in the attempt.

Then what meaning shall the evangelist point out in the Cross so that it will become the means of my being crucified to the world in order that I may receive new life? Why, no meaning at all but the objection itself: the stumbling block becomes the cornerstone. Perhaps the way to the most pointed answer is to come boldly through the strength of the attackers.

Bernard Shaw argued:

Every man to whom salvation is offered has an inalienable natural right to say "No, thank you: I prefer to retain my full moral responsibility: it is not good for me to be able to load a scapegoat with my sins: I should be less careful how I committed them if I knew they would cost me nothing." Then, too, there is the attitude of Ibsen . . . to whom the whole scheme of salvation was only an ignoble attempt to cheat God; to get into heaven without paying the price.[2]

[2] George Bernard Shaw, *op. cit.* By permission of The Public Trustee and the Society of Authors.

Whatever he may have left unsaid about how man comes to be endowed with the "inalienable natural right to say 'No, thank you,'" Shaw was right to insist on man's free moral responsibility. And although it is the shortest road to phariseeism, the context shows that his argument was intended as an antidote to antinomianism, which is the disease of flaunting immorality in the face of grace. But the point missed is the crucial point: having for oneself no price with which to pay sin's cost or heaven's fee, that admission of poverty itself is, in fact, the greatest possible price one can pay. The admission price to the kingdom is the admission of complete inability to pay any price. It happens also to be the surrender of any attempt by one's own power to assert one's identity independently from God.

In man's refusal to permit Christ to take his place is found the last ditch of rebellion. If even his guilt is taken away, there is at last in truth nothing left but the life God gives. Faith is to accept the fact of forgiveness.

> Could my tears forever flow,
> Could my zeal no languor know,
> These for sin could not atone;
> Thou must save, and Thou alone:
> In my hand no price I bring;
> Simply to Thy cross I cling.

> —AUGUSTUS M. TOPLADY

Thus, with acceptance of God's love comes deliverance from the powers of idolatry and sin.

Although the structure of this book has brought us at this point to a consideration of the Cross as the means of our acceptance of Christ's invitation, we must not suppose that the work of evangelism proceeds with any such super-imposed precision. The old "natural" self is a hydra and must be crucified moment by moment always; a man must die daily and be born daily. It would probably be equally mistaken to imagine that outside a book any man's behavior was ever all pure acceptance. God's revelation elicits alternating and mixed response and resistance. There-fore, the work of evangelism, because dynamic, must be continuous and must be applied, not point by point, but as a whole process along that whole process called person-ality.

It is because Jesus is the "total abolitionist of all previous claims on our confidence" that we have seen him to be; and because the coming into life requires a change this radical—that is, the absolute eradication of the present counterfeit self—it is for these reasons that Christian evangelism must be evangelism in depth. Evangelism which does not center in the Cross is at best superficial and proba-bly a brand of idolatry. If the Cross is taken lightly, as a fetish, forgotten as an instrument of death and brandished instead as a symbol of superiority, it has merely been degraded to the level of an idol's trophy—something we use instead of something God uses.

In this connection it is worth observing that in the index to Schneider and Dornbusch's recent analysis, *Popular Reli-gion*,[3] the words "Cross" and "Atonement" do not even appear. The omission does not necessarily mean that these ideas are absent from all the forty-six religious best sellers analyzed by the sociologists, but it does indicate that in their study, the Cross as the means of salvation does not

---

[3] Louis Schneider and Sanford M. Dornbusch, *Popular Religion* (Chicago: The University of Chicago Press, 1958).

show up as an overstressed feature in the religiosity presumed to be permeating our society. It may also go to explain the feelings which moved one preacher to title a sermon: "Don't Talk Cross to Me!" This reluctance to face the Cross—reflecting a reluctance to face the depth of human sin and idolatry because of a deeper reluctance to face what is feared to be human powerlessness and helplessness—is the challenge of evangelism.

If Christianity is to be taken seriously, repentance and conversion must mean more than merely tooting the horn in polite and chummy salute as merrily we roll along down our own broad and easy ways to destruction: they must mean turning back and turning around at the Cross. Decision must mean more than being beaten into formal assent with the shillelagh of shame in the eyes of one's children to rise to the level of the statistical majority: it must mean free and dangerous determination even though it be a cross. Salvation must mean more than a new name on a dotted line; it must mean a new life in the kingdom of God whose standard is the Cross. If Christianity is to have its saving impact and be more than a palliative, then without neglecting the extensive evangelism of popular religion, Christan evangelists must rededicate themselves to the intensive depth evangelism of the Cross. If we cannot take up the Cross, we can neither extend nor accept the invitation of Christ.

Superficial evangelism—if the term is allowable—may produce a "lift" or a "warm glow"; but evangelism centered in the Cross produces exaltation. Because it reveals God's power, his gracious love for sinners, and his forgiveness of penitents, the Cross, signifying God's acceptance of us, becomes the means of our acceptance of his invitation and, therefore, the cause for our rejoicing.

To those for whom all this "Cross talk" is morbid, unpleasant, and "ugly as sin," it cannot but seem strange, almost shocking, to find disciples behaving so merrily at "the place which is called The Skull." Their protest at this incongruous joy is almost an echo of the words of scandalized reproach which were leveled at Jesus and his disciples for eating and drinking instead of praying and fasting. Unseemly to revel and be joyful at the Cross? For those who have found there the perfection of divine love, no other attitude is appropriate: "earth's blackest day" is also a Good Friday. At Calvary they still eat and drink to their souls' health; and the bridegroom is still with them.

How shall the evangelist persuade men to come to this victory celebration for life, to grasp the means by which they, too, may participate in it and accept the invitaton of Christ?

10

METHODS OF GAINING ACCEPTANCE

Just as the techniques which we employ in order to gain acceptance of Christ's invitation imply a certain understanding of evangelism, so our conception of evangelism dictates the use of appropriate methods while it rules out others. The nature of our message must determine the nature of our methods. This is the proper order. Too often we confront, or are confronted by, our fellow workmen with ready-cut die-cast methods buttressed here and there with a flying rationale, as if these tools existed in their own right and for their own sake, as if our best theology and our best evangelism had nothing to do with each other.

As a result of having welcomed perfectly good wooden horses, some evangelists unwittingly violate the integrity of the church. The verbal distinction between words such as "evangelist" and "pastor" is allowed to become a source of actual conflict within a minister. A layman forces himself to go through a pattern of behavior which may give the lie to his true feelings and beliefs, and thus disqualify himself as a sincere evangelist while he learns with all of its attendant feelings duplicity in the name of discipleship. Another result may be seen in the rate of fall-off among relatively new converts insofar as it indicates a man's disenchanting recognition of the disparity between the life he has entered and the sign he had read on the door.

Thinking through the processes of evangelism together, we have had frequent opportunities to ask whether our practice was a consistent and effective way of implementing our understanding of what evangelism is. We have made no attempt to separate practice from theory—the direct opposite has been our aim and assertion—and we intend no such division now as we turn specifically to the question of methods. But in our day, when packaged programs of tested techniques join with soaring church membership statistics to shout that evangelism is successful, we are merely fulfilling our responsibility when we examine our procedures and the content they imply. We have tried to interweave these threads; now, on the basis of our discussion to this point, let us draw together in explicit form some of the more important criteria by which we may evaluate our practice as evangelists.

First, the evangelist will use only methods which are consistent with and motivated by the spirit of love and the mandate of Christ. This means that the passion the evangelist must have for souls is a holy passion; he is concerned for people for the right reason. The Lord's calling is "gracious," and evangelism's motive is to give—to give good news, to give life; not to give in order to get. Each potential convert is to be looked upon, not as a feather

113

for the evangelist's cap and not as a star for his crown, but as a brother-child to be restored to their Father and his family. If we are correct in speaking of Spirit as immeasurable, then it is a ridiculous procedure to count converts in order to measure evangelism, unless the purpose of counting be to discover the missing. We must guard against treating members of Christ's body as replaceable parts and summing up their significance in a statistic. Let an evangelist hitch his wagon to a chart or be motivated by pride and its desires to appear "successful," and his aim will seem to justify any method by which he can procure new adherents as trophies. Our God is not success. We follow one who in the wilderness refused the temptation to gain a following by falling down before sure-fire methods and who refused to place the words of God at the service of idols. All of which is only to say that the evangelist must be a person who is himself responding to Christ's calling—and, by implication, that the vocation of every such person is to be an evangelist.

In addition to making certain that his methods are adopted for the right reason, the evangelist must take care that the methods he uses present the right invitation. He must communicate the invitation intact—as Christ's free call for all men to join with him in a personal relationship of following in which they become sharers of life, of possessions, and in the celebration of God.

We have already seen how a method inconsistent with the motive of evangelism distorts the invitation. The evangelist must faithfully reproduce the invitation without other distortions caused by preconceptions—his own, or those held by the invited—of what a pleasant invitation should sound like. He dare not insist that discipleship conform to his own patterns. Whom Christ welcomes, he welcomes; what Christ commends, he commends. His purpose is not to supplant Christ as mediator, but to bring all men directly to Christ. Any evangelistic effort, therefore, must express our faith that God is able to meet with equal sufficiency each of the infinite varieties of human experience. Evangelistic procedures which are based on the assumption that one narrow band of techniques will be adequate equipment for dealing with every or the same individual in every condition will deny that Christ's invitation is really for all men, will deny God's ability to save each and all, and will win only those who can be won by this particular approach. It is like assuming that because tuna can be caught in a large mesh, therefore all fish can be caught in a large mesh. But not all fish are tuna; and neither will a fragile net catch a sailfish. Further, such rigid use of prefabricated evangelism will result in a stagnant uniformity within the church which will in turn reinforce the restricted preconceptions of that evangelism: "All the fish in here are tuna; that proves all fish are tuna; therefore the way to catch all fish is to use the same sort of net that caught these," and so make the church more and more ingrown. Because the kind of churches we have depends largely on the kind of evangelism we practice, our evangelistic methods must dare to follow the Spirit.

Since man's acceptance of God's gracious offer in Christ can be effected only when reconciliation in Christ has been accepted, the evangelist must deal with men in a radical way. He may not allow the invitation to be garbled by ingenious subterfuge or made shallow by superficial response. With relentless penetration he will present the invitation in its full depth. And because he cannot abet corruption of the invitation by pretending that God's love is only for individuals and not for the world, the evangelist will also be the ambassador-statesman, dealing with rebellious society in a regeneratively revolutionary way.

This sort of evangelistic practice—varied, broad, penetrating—requires courage. Lack of daring may account for much of our ineffectiveness, including that falling back on anachronistic procedures which, however they may twist the evangel and fail in reaching many, are at least safe from criticism behind the sacrosanct vestments of custom and the "good old days." Probably the best evangelistic methods will never be tools which can be applied to a situation by any mechanic who can read the instruction manual, but instead will be methods which arise inside the situation itself simply from the attempt to confront the man as he is with God's call. That is, they will not be methods to be imposed upon, but methods which will enable the process of evangelism to take place within the processes of life. Therefore, we do not propose here to add to the technical armory of the evangelist but, rather, to point to the courage needed to take our evangelism into those situations where the techniques will be demanded and where the Spirit will give utterance.

At the same time, remembering that he holds this treasure in an earthen vessel—a "vessel in which the sediment of sin transforms the wine of knowledge given by God into the vinegar of idolatry" [1]—the evangelist may well doubt whether he is ever able to speak the invitation without some adulteration, much less to assure its full communication. Because of this, he will proffer it with

[1] Herbert H. Farmer, *Revelation and Religion* (New York: Harper & Brothers, 1954), p. 40.

humility, but he will not pervert that virtue by permitting his humility to tie his tongue altogether. Confident that evangelism is the work of God's love, he need sound no uncertain trumpet. The difference is in being certain of God while being uncertain of himself.

The most serious threat of distortion lies in methods which would accommodate the invitation to the willfulness of the guests. The ambassador for Christ must never permit his desire to grant peace with God to the kingdoms and citizens of this world to tempt him into concessions and the conclusion of an ignominious truce through appeasement. He has not been sent to surrender in the name of God. His problem is how to be at once courageous and cordial. The evangelist is constrained by the love of Christ to persuade men; yet some men are offended by the love of Christ. This is the rack which the ministry of reconciliation involves. To be loyal to Christ, faithfully to represent his invitation, and yet not to persuade men, is to fall somewhat short of what we aimed at—especially if we believe that loyalty to Christ involves persuading men. But to succeed at persuading men and, in order to do it, to be disloyal to Christ and to misrepresent God by accommodating our message to itching ears is utterly to fail, is to persuade men to something other than loyalty to Christ. We must seek to persuade men, and we must please God.

This tension in which the evangelist is privileged to share the suffering of Christ is inescapable. In order to curb any tendency to resolve it, we must apply to evangelistic methods a third criterion: the evangelist must preserve the structure of decision.

This means that the evangelist will bring decision to the level of full awareness. To accept this obligation is to accept a challenge—particularly when the evangelist is the educator—to make presentation of the issues involved much sharper than can be done by mere accumulation of assertions and experiences, until commitment will supersede conditioning. The evangelist seeks a decision—favorable if possible; but just as he will risk refusal rather than betray his trust, so he will prefer a negative decision to engineered consent.

Put baldly, the attempt in methods of manipulation is to secure a conditioned response by triggering an overmastering though hidden psychological need or personality deficiency over which the subject cannot or does not exercise conscious control. The effort is not to solve a problem but to exploit it—some would even say to create the problem for exploitation.

Presumably techniques are now available, and some of them in use, by which the evangelist may soul-wash any given individual if not in the blood of the Lamb, then in contrived revivals and manufactured movements. We can manipulate all comers into morality—at least, into church membership—by touching them at their points of desire for prestige (status with family, community, and self), for conformity, for poise, for confidence. We can sell and sell out Christianity if we take advantage of the phenomenon of anxiety buying. Self-justification is easy: we must be wise as serpents, ready to match skills with the children of darkness. But we had better ask ourselves whether acting on the belief that man is an object to be manipulated is quite the harmless activity of a dove. The objective of evangelism must be men created anew by God and responding to him in love and freedom. If the churches manipulate men to conform to preselected goals, will they not find that they have at that same instant destroyed the goal?

Although we have insisted on the social orientation of evangelism, we do not overlook the dangers of social coercion whereby a man wears a cross for the same reason that he wears a necktie, or calls himself Christian either because it is the popular thing to do or because it never occurred to him that anything else was possible.

If we gain acceptance of Christ's invitation by manipulating a man into the position where he serves God unwittingly, we have brought our Father a zombie, not a living son raised from the dead.

The evangelist's concern is not to manipulate motives in order to achieve some desired result. His desired result is precisely this: to purify these very motives themselves so that a man may seek the kingdom of God first. He is not trying to get him to do the right thing for the wrong reason but, so far as possible, the right thing for the right reason—above all for the right reason, purity of heart.

Again the objection may be raised: "Since we tend to defend what 'I' do as right simply because I do it, then isn't there something to be said for manipulating a man into doing a thing so that he will as a result persuade himself, just as he learns to believe in Christ by following Christ?" In distinction from the self-verification of faith, the motive proposed here for his persuasion of himself is self-justification; and it is just the motive we are aiming at. He will have become persuaded simply because he is still a slave to self, and in that slavery with our encouragement he will remain.

In *King Lear*, in the stage's most brutal scene, Gloucester's eyes are gouged out. The blinded old man enlists a guide to lead him toward the cliffs of Dover where he intends to destroy himself. Along the way they are met by Edgar, the son whom Gloucester—mistakenly believing Edgar plotted his murder—had disowned. Keeping his identity secret, Edgar takes the guide's place. He brings his father to a small hillock and tells him that they are now standing at the precipice of the cliffs. Gloucester leaps and falls a few feet, uninjured.

Shakespeare has here given us a picture of despair's leap in the dark; and it is just that—a leap of despair and not of faith. What we are concerned with now is the son's deception in order to cure his father's despair and preserve his life.

No doubt there are evangelists who lead the blind to a ditch and call it the precipice of faith. They let their charges down easy, and the old "natural" man believes his life has been saved. But that is not the innocent use of improper methods: that is charlatanism.

If we imagine a man poised on the brink of faith, we can question what our own role as guide is. If we wheedle him by telling him that all he must do is take the first step, we had better warn him that the first step is a long one. If we entice him over the edge by jingling gold before him and tell him that all this will be added unto him if he first steps out, his stepping out will not be in order to free himself from Mammon. If we can stretch our fancy further and imagine that our would-be leaper into faith is standing on an electric grid like those used to condition experimental animals with jolts, and then imagine ourselves pushing the button, our subject may leap like an inspired gazelle. Noting the result with satisfaction, we may mark the experiment a success and boast that he even surpassed the goal. But we can hardly call it a leap of faith. It may be more certain than deceiving the blind at a ditch; it may generate more distance than a shove; but the principle is the same: faith was nowhere near it.

Methods of manipulation which, in order to reduce the amount of the evangelist's risk of "failure," violate the structure of decision and destroy man by depriving him of freedom, not only confess the evangelist's lack of daring, but are also the flat denial of faith and the very opposite of what we mean by evangelism. Evangelism is a dynamic process in which something happens (a relationship is established and experienced) between persons mutually. The evangelist does not do something to a subject; both participate in a communication of God's Word, which speaks to the evangelist as much as to the convert. Therefore: "We have renounced disgraceful, underhanded ways; we refuse to practice cunning or to tamper with God's word, but by the open statement of the truth we would commend ourselves to every man's conscience in the sight of God" (II Cor. 4:2).

Evangelistic methods should spring from and be appropriate to the controlling love of Christ; they should present Christ's calling without tampering; they should preserve the structure of decision. And they should meet as a fourth test this check on the third: the methods by which the evangelist seeks to gain acceptance for the invitation of Christ, if they are to create man in his free existence before God, must be persuasive methods.

In analyzing the structure of decision in Chapter 5, we saw that Christ confronted Peter with an alternative to sin's bondage. We also saw that in thus confronting Peter with the demand, "Follow me," far from violating Peter's

121

personality by exerting undue pressure, Christ actually placed Peter in real freedom to choose and thereby placed him in real manhood. It follows that refusal to persuade—that is, refusal to offer real choice—is what denies the dignity of man and deprives him of the opportunity to define himself and to have a self through decision before God.

There is a delicate line beyond which freedom of speech becomes license to exploit, and the evangelist must be careful not to fall over it. When, instead of being used to encourage choice, persuasion is used to subvert it, then it has become manipulation. But there is an equally dangerous line where refusal to exercise persuasion becomes a conspiracy of silence against freedom. The servant of the king is sent to strongly urge the guests to come in.

Any man who sees his brother in the path of a truck has an obligation to persuade: failure to do everything in human power to save him is to consent to his death. If, of his own free choice, the brother then wheels and plunges back into the street to his deliberate death, the story is complicated, but love's obligation is not lessened. Berdyaev speaks of man as both a king and a slave—and as neither, truly free.[2] Man is a slave because slavery is easy. He is horrified with "the fearful burden of free choice": the responsibilities and the risks of freedom are too great. Man runs about trying to find some authority to take it off his hands. Morally, that is, he wishes not to be. Freedom when not exercised becomes slavery, and man would like to commit this spiritual suicide. So he is easy to manipulate, for one thing, because being manipulated is easier for him.

[2] Nicolas Berdyaev, *Slavery and Freedom* (New York: Charles Scribner's Sons, 1944), Part I, ch. 2, pp. 59-72.

But though his willful brother dart back out into the easy way of destruction and stretch himself out before the juggernaut, the one thing the evangelist will not do in order to stop him is to shoot him at the curb. And though it is offered as a button to push, manipulation is really a trigger to squeeze. To say that the evangelist will use all sorts of nets to catch all sorts of men in all sorts of conditions is not the same as saying that he will catch them dead or alive.

The persuader, by refusing to dictate and by keeping live choice always confronting man, keeps decision, freedom, and soul alive. It is to accomplish this result that we persuade men. Not to control what a man does with his freedom—thus destroying it and him, not to control what a man does with the grace God offers him in Christ—however urgently we feel obligated to express our hope that he will grasp it in faith, but in persuading to face man with freedom, with its inward illumination, grace, with life. Confrontation with the inviting Christ gives man something to choose besides death. Without that choice he is not free and not fully man. Without that challenge he is incapable of response before God, and to be incapable of response is to be dead.

Perhaps it is impossible for us ever entirely to free our methods of evangelism from the taint of manipulation. Some of the factors which unintentionally influence without creating conscious decision are so subtle that they escape our power to keep them all under control. Our best remedy is to sharpen our persuasion, to present Christ in all his winsomeness, to let our lives and our words speak his challenge so clearly that no man shall be able not to make his own decision, not to take his place for that moment of existence before God as a child, rebellious or responsive.

Thus we have a fifth criterion for evaluating evangelistic methods: they must be effective. They must work, they must succeed on the Lord's terms. We will not use any method simply because it is effective; we dare not use any method unless it is effective. Being the means by which we translate our belief about God's love into patterns of human action, we cannot dismiss them as "mere" techniques. No aid or comfort should be taken by those whose practice of evangelism is ineffective; no one is by this understanding released from pressing his efforts to the last jot and tittle. However adroitly a Christian's evangelistic work steers between the pitfalls, if it does not meet men on the highways and byways and strongly urge them to come in, then it fails.

There is no question but that our evangelism ought to "produce results." Our question now is: What results?

RESULTS OF ACCEPTANCE

That minister who, as the nominal head of a legal corporation, received a questionnaire designed for the manufacturing firms of his city and proceded to answer its question "What product do you make?" with the word "People" showed a good sense of proportion as well as a sense of humor. Answering a questionnaire is like carrying on a conversation through a keyhole. Given the chance, no doubt that minister would have wished to expand his answer beyond the space allowed. He might have wanted to explain that since his "firm" produced people, nothing human was outside its scope; that everything, including factories, that affected the quality of people was his business. He might have wanted to sketch in the characteristics of the personalities he felt it his concern to produce.

Granted he does not pretend to accomplish it by his own power, how shall we describe the "new creature" who is the intended fruit of the evangelist's work?

The minimum objective for the evangelist is to produce persons. Believing that a man exists as true man only in the free acceptance of the risk of choosing his own direction when arrested by the gracious calling of the Lord, the evangelist seeks a reaction—favorable or unfavorable—by placing men within the structure of decision in regard to the invitation of Christ. Even before asking the question he most loves, "Was a decision made for Christ?" the evangelist must ask, "Was a decision made?" To produce reaction before God is to produce a person. After that he asks, "Did this person choose life or death?"

From this conception of evangelism as a continuously dynamic process—and our consequent insistence that the risk of faith shall be kept alive by the interplay of the possibilities of resistance and response—it can be seen first that the evangelist never arrives at a "finished" product, and second that one of the dominant characteristics that the evangelist desires for the person he persuades is the quality best called spontaneity.

Since the most obvious thing death means is the incapacity to make response, one of the primary hallmarks of a man raised from death to newness of life is the spontaneous life of the Spirit. The evangelist is concerned that the person he wins choose to continue to live, that he choose to continue becoming a person by continually responding to Christ.

Consider the picture a man presents when he has no life within him, no inner self-determination, and, therefore, no self. His life is governed from without: he lives after the flesh, forever seeking outside stimulation—attaching batteries to the leg of a dead frog so that, mistaking a twitching of the nerves for a living response, he may delude himself with the reassuring appearance of life. A man controlled by idols is not free to give except where he hopes to get, to value a thing or to like a person except where he hopes for advantage to himself. All that he does is not what he wills, but what his pride dictates. He is pinned down with the strings of petty social, economic, and moral inhibitions, things he does or refrains from doing, not because he wants to, but because he must, until he is like Gulliver in Lilliput in a thousand small ways immobilized and irresponsive.

But the Spirit of the Lord brings freedom. Whereas the life contained in idols is like a stagnant pool, the life of free inner determination is pictured by Jesus in the image of a spring: "The water that I shall give him will become in him a spring of water welling up to eternal life" (John 4:14). What is so spontaneous as a spring? A well is deliberately dug and shaped by hard labor, an artificial imitation of a spring; and its water must be drawn or forced up. A reservoir is made to hold what it is given, to store up and release the liquid as it is needed. But the nature of a spring is to flow, to overflow, to pour out unstintingly, freely, making the land fruitful with its prodigality, its water always fresh. Not all springs are alike. Some leap spectacularly; others flow gently and hidden. But all flow of themselves, independently of exterior surface conditions, proceeding from and giving evidence of a deep source, tapping some unseen, inexhaustible supply. A spring is true to its nature, joyously free. This is the character of the kingdom life. The source within man is cleansed and purified. His behavior is no gutter from a sewer; what flows up is love, and man loves and does as he pleases. For "out of his heart shall flow rivers of living water" (John 7:38). When, because evangelism has met him at the root of his being, all his acts, attitudes, and achievements are meant to express the creative will of God, they are truly his own, and he is God's and God's life lives within him.

Another characteristic of the person evangelism seeks to produce in response to the invitation of Christ is the dual quality of wholeness and full participation in life.

In ancient Rome the poet Catullus composed this invitation:

Fabullus, come to dinner at my house, but bring your own food, a pretty girl and wit, if you want a good time. For my purse is full of cobwebs. I shall give you my affection, and a rare exquisite perfume belonging to Lesbia. When you smell it, you will pray to become all nose.[1]

If the Roman nose is not the answer to a prayer to perfume, the spiritual principles are nevertheless true: that we tend to become like what we worship, or man is what he follows. Wrong worship and wrong prayer produce distorted personalities.[2]

The technique of the cartoonist is to exaggerate one or a few features of his subject until the part identifies the whole. There is a sense in which the life of each of us can be caricatured in this manner. We have one long and strong suit we have to play, or preference leads us to develop along a narrow band, or else circumstances demand that we major in this one thing. But, suggests Lawrence Langner,[3] this restricts us from full participation in life. He believes that a man ought to have multiple professions, a sort of life-long vocation in liberal arts. If we agree in theory, the fact remains that an important strategic element in personal

---

[1] Catullus. Occasional poem No. 13.

[2] Gilkey, *op. cit.*, p. 196.

[3] Lawrence Langner, *The Magic Curtain* (New York: E. P. Dutton and Company, 1951), p. 445.

management is concentration of force. And most of us, while we may hold the line in other areas, mass for a break-through at one point. There is a division of labor because there is a diversity of gifts. The Middle Ages' ideal of the encyclopedic man has given way to the need for the specialist. The poverty which we, with Mr. Langner, abhor comes when our particular gift prevents us from full participation in life. It may be said to be the "hell-mark" of an idol that, like a cancer, its worship gives nourishment to one part of a man at the cost of destroying the other parts and therefore the whole, and that directed to an idol, prayer results in partial living and therefore total death.

Having tasted the water of life, a man prays to become all life. At the kingdom party we recognize and rejoice in diversity. But there the partial life becomes part of the complete and universal life of Christ, life which is neither limited nor limiting.

"Christians, Incorporated." This is the sign of the kingdom-life and the objective of evangelism. Jesus called his disciples branches of the vine. Paul, who could at times use that same language, went from plant life to human life and, in what may be the most strikingly bold image ever conceived, called participants in the gospel members of the body of Christ. Each differentiated, each limited, all make one body and apart from it they have no life. Sin is separation, the eye saying it has no need of the hand— asserting its true independence of function as a false independence of existence. Idolatry is the foot saying to the body, "You exist to serve me." But the purpose of Christ's incarnation is incorporation. He became flesh that men might become members of his body and of one another. It is not that a disciple becomes the entire life of the body, but, rather, that he participates fully in all the life of the body of which he is a part.

When sin's separation is overcome in the body of Christ, men of diverse temperaments, abilities, and gifts share one Spirit. Harmony—not necessarily unison—replaces discord; consuming ambition is transformed to constructive aspiration; voracious rivalry is transmuted to that amiable contest in which all "strive to excel in building up the church" (I Cor. 14:12). The members complement and supplement one another and are all one life. As two eyes see from different angles and blend their vision to accurate seeing, as muscle pulls against muscle to make movement, as the thumb opposed to the fingers enables the hand to hold, so the Church with diversity has unity. This indivisible body of Christ cannot suffer the amputations of geography, time, or denomination. This community itself undertakes the healing work of evangelism among mankind. Evangelism is the work of the church and all that we say of the evangelist we must say of the church.

Integrally related and analagous to full participation in life is the quality of wholeness which evangelism aims to produce within the person himself. The war within a man's own body between impulses urging him in many directions despite his desire to follow Christ is to be changed from the rioting of a mob to the power of a disciplined battalion. Not that the many-sided personality shall be rubbed to a dull sameness, but that each facet shall refract the light of Christ. Within the person there will still be many men, often opposed; tensions will still rise among them; but the resultant will not be disintegration, but dynamic decisions for Christ.

Jesus promises this life of connection in his great invitation:

Come to me, all who labor and are heavy-laden, and I will give you rest. Take my yoke upon you, and learn from me; for I am gentle and lowly in heart, and you will find rest for your souls. For my yoke is easy, and my burden is light.—MATT. 11:28-30

Yoked by the love of Christ, even forces pulling man apart, so long as they remain within one yoke, find their opposition pulling forward. For man, as for men, this joining is the secret of harnessing otherwise destructive forces for the fulfillment of life's purposes. It is also the secret of power: to have a resting place—a place of traction —from which to expend energy along the line of purpose. But there is no power unless there is resistance against which energy gains purchase. The follower is related directly to the life of his own time; his discipleship demands of him definite actions; his own body and the larger one of which he is fully a part exert power in the world to redeem it. Thus we find that the person evangelism desires to produce is a man possesed of responsibilities and burdens other men do not have—and possessed, too, by that power and purpose which, for making burdens light, is more than sufficient.

A person whose behavior springs spontaneously from one pure motive, who finds fulfillment for his limited life in full participation in the life of Christ, a person made whole by the yoke of his first love and with all the energies of mind, heart, soul, and strength gathered and directed with power for God's purposes—this person is the result evangelism intends to produce. These fruits testify to the work of the Spirit; these qualities will not be burnt away in testing fire; these characteristics bespeak the effectiveness of our evangelism. As if to give the mark of his own approval to man's loving response, on this new creation God sets his seal of joy.

Whenever a new creation has beheld its Lord, it has burst out in singing. With Tertullian the saints of the centuries testify that the Holy Spirit is a glad spirit. Kierkegaard sends syllables somersaulting to the tune: "I rejoice over my joy, of, in, by, at, on, through, with my joy"! For the new man anointed with the oil of gladness, the very universe itself is reborn and all things are become new-made. When he goes out attired in his new wedding garment for the feast, he goes out with joy and is led forth with peace. He hears the morning stars singing together to celebrate our God. The mountains and the hills and their springs of laughing water break forth before him into singing echoes of the song in his soul, and all the trees of the field clap their hands. Bearing this mark of joy, infinitely different from and greater than any other joy man may know, none may convince the new creature that he is not the work of God's hand.

All this for the man the evangelist calls! And shall not the worthy laborer himself have his hire? He would be more than content with the lowest seat at the table. The King rewards him who serves not for reward. It is in this same glad spirit that the evangelist—and who, having heard this song, could hold back from singing it aloud?— does his work. The greatest single drag on his own gladness is that it and all other fruits of the Spirit are not freely shared by all—and to that extent his own remains incomplete. Not all the guests are come; the servant is sent for others, that the house may be filled and that joy may be full. It is to this glad celebration of the Spirit that the evangelist, in Christ's own stead, invites the wanderer. It is for the sheer joy of seeing men rejoicing come to exultant life that in season and out he is diligent to make known the gracious calling of the Lord.

> Joy is the wine that God is ever pouring
> Into the hearts of those who strive with Him,
> Light'ning their eyes to vision and adoring,
> Strength'ning their arms to warfare glad and grim.

—G. A. STUDDERT-KENNEDY[4]

It is true that often enough he does his work patiently and painfully; true that often enough he has to chorus his thanksgiving for a lifetime's passion even when his quest seems fruitless and long; true that often enough he feels like a voice sending a "burst of music down an un-listening street." But if it is also true that Christ is the Son of God; if it is true that Christ is the Word of God, the very incarnation of the ultimate meaning at the heart of the universe through whom the universe was created, in whom the universe coheres, and by whom the universe is salvaged from meaningless futility, helplessness, and hope-lessness; then evangelism is faith's first and finest work. If this faith is true, then in what the herald of good news does there is an unsurpassed glory. The evangelist seeks no song for himself—only a hymn to God. Nevertheless, Stephen Spender has made the song for him:

[4] G. A. Studdert-Kennedy, "The Suffering God," from *The Unutterable Beauty* (New York: Harper & Brothers, 1936). By permission of Harper & Brothers and Hodder & Stoughton, Ltd.

133

I think continually of those who were truly great.
Who, from the womb, remembered the soul's history
Through corridors of light where the hours are suns
Endless and singing. Whose lovely ambition
Was that their lips, still touched with fire,
Should tell of the Spirit clothed from head to foot in song.[5]

[5] From *Poems by Stephen Spender*. Copyright 1934 by Modern Library, Inc.; published by Random House. Used by permission of Random House and Faber and Faber, Ltd.

INDEX

141